OUR LAST
TWO THOUSAND YEARS

AN IRISHWOMAN'S
HISTORY OF ENGLAND

EILEEN MURPHY

LOVAT DICKSON *&* THOMPSON **LIMITED**
PUBLISHERS
LONDON

FIRST PUBLISHED 1935

LOVAT DICKSON AND THOMPSON LIMITED
38 BEDFORD STREET LONDON AND ST MARTIN'S HOUSE
BOND STREET TORONTO

SET AND PRINTED IN GREAT BRITAIN BY
LATIMER TREND AND COMPANY MOUNT PLEASANT PLYMOUTH

Contents

CONTENTS

CONTENTS

Illustrations

9

Acknowledgements are due to the Great Western Railway for the pictures of Glastonbury Abbey Ruins, facing page 88, and the Village Scene, facing page 51.

Preface

I AM a Kilkenny woman and I like English people. I have always wondered at the contrast between the Irish and the English—a contrast of customs, manners, habits of thought, beliefs and hopes. The racial ingredients of the two nations being much alike, I felt that the roots of the difference between them must be found in their history. So I began to read Irish history; but it was impossible to understand without a knowledge of English history too. Now the English history I had learned at school—dates of battles, lists of kings and trumpery anecdotes—was worse than useless from this point of view. I wanted a connected narrative of the development of the English people, told in understandable modern terms and appraising the great men and great movements of history by modern standards. I wanted to trace the terrific effects of religious change on domestic and foreign politics, on social and economic life, on national thought and feeling. Above all, as an active participant in modern life and not an exponent of university scholarship, I wanted this history told in plain simple language for people like myself; and I could not find it.

In these circumstances I determined to write my own history of England. For its scholarly tinge I am indebted to the historical researches of my friend T. W. Coghlin. The reasoning and conclusions are my own. Reader, proceed!

EILEEN MURPHY

ON an August afternoon two thousand years ago, Julius Cæsar disembarked his troops at Deal. They grounded their galleys and waded ashore against a charge of British chariots. This was the first Roman invasion of England.

Fifty years later Jesus Christ was born in the eastern part of the Roman Empire.

With these two facts the recorded history of England begins. In essence it is the local variant of a greater theme: the rise, dominion and decline of Christian civilization in the western world.

OUR LAST
TWO THOUSAND YEARS

England in the Year One

WHEN Christ was born, England was still un-conquered by the Romans. Cæsar's two landings had been nothing more than military bluff, calculated to alarm these barbarian neighbours of romanized France.

Britons might be barbarians by Roman stan-dards, but they were not cannibals or cavemen. They lived in clans like the Scottish Highlanders, under a chieftain or king. Their priests were Druids, who preached the immortality of the soul, offered human sacrifices, and practised the art of magic; in the last two respects they were like some modern doctors. The hanging of mistletoe at Christmas is a survival of Druid practice, though possibly the rites performed under the mistletoe have changed.

The Britons were Celts by race, like Ramsay MacDonald, David Lloyd George, and myself. Their clans were not nomadic like American

Indians; they had settled villages for farming, reared cattle, grew corn, and mined tin for export. They had a good name as breeders of sporting dogs, and were heavy drinkers of mead, which was still a favourite tipple among Thomas Hardy's rustics eighty years ago.

In addition, the coast-living Britons were traders in a small way. They often crossed the Channel to do business with the French. Now France had been conquered and made into a Roman province; but before she was subdued, some of the Britons fought for their French friends against the legions. This was the real reason for Cæsar's military demonstrations in Britain. The Romans, like the British to-day, knew that there will always be trouble when a conquered province is bordered by an irresponsible race who have never known the blessings of civilization, and still less its burdens, which at that time included heavy taxation, conscription, and intensified legal slavery.

Between Cæsar's landings and the Roman conquest, the Southern Britons kept up their dealings with France. Roman merchants crossed the Channel in their turn, bringing their lingo with their wares. Englishmen began to pick up the Roman language and Roman ways of life. Some of the British kings even struck coins with Latin

The British Empire depends for its life on sea connections guarded by battleships

The Roman Empire depended for its life on walls and roads, which fell into decay long ago

inscriptions, an unquestionable sign of the spreading influence of the Empire.

Roman Empire and British Empire

AT the time of Christ's birth, Augustus ruled the Roman Empire. This empire comprised Italy, North Africa, Spain, France, the Balkans, the Mediterranean islands, Greece, and Asia Minor. Under the Roman Empire, Europe became an efficiently governed United States, but with no nonsense about liberty and equality.

The Empire was gripped together by the Roman Army, of which the Emperor himself was the head. This army was carefully recruited, subjected to an iron discipline and kept continually on active service at the frontiers. It was something more than the armies of to-day, because its commanders were political governors and civil engineers as well as professional soldiers.

They supervised the making of the great Roman roads, built across every kind of country to link up the garrison cities and to serve as trade routes for all the Empire. Just as the British Empire depends for its life on sea-connections, the Roman Empire depended on its army and its roads.

The Roman army kept the peace in Europe. It was a sort of uncorrupted international police force. In this capacity it put an end to tribal skirmishes and cut-throat little wars, so that farming, mining, trade and the arts had scope to thrive; and in every imperial province the Roman law (still widely used to-day) was superimposed on local custom and tribal habit, and controlled all the activities of Roman citizens including trade, religion and industry.

The Roman Peace had to be paid for; the price was a tribute of grain, of metal, and of slaves.

In this military Empire, as in the capitalist civilization of to-day, the lives of the rich were in marked contrast to the lives of the poor. The town-houses and manor-houses of the rich were fitted with air-heating systems and baths and tesselated pavings; there was a constant supply of luxurious food and wine; and many of those who had inherited wealth without responsibility were unproductive gluttons, drunkards, and sensualists. Others were philosophers and connoisseurs of art and letters. Others again, with energy and ambition, were soldiers and administrators, identifying their careers with the Roman mission to bring peace and order over all the known world, and firmly fixing the idea of European unity which was to prevail for fifteen hundred years.

All these types could be duplicated in a London club to-day. The cocktail-swilling Mayfair lounger; the rowdy young Guardsman; the cleverish dilettante whose work is never quite first-rate; the dyspeptic financier; the lawyer with political ambitions; the capable but unimaginative civil servant; the yellow-eyed Colonial Governor home on leave; all these had their counterparts in the Rome of Augustus.

Slavery too Expensive in the Long Run

THE basis of this society was slavery. All the manual work was done by slaves. They worked the land, built and staffed the houses, mined the metals, oared the galleys and quarried the stone. There were different degrees of slavery, and the treatment of slaves varied widely. At one end of the scale were the educated slaves, treated kindly like housedogs, who tutored their young masters; at the other end were the labourers who worked in convict gangs under the lash and slept in fetid subterranean dens.

Superficially, slavery has the important advantage of cheapness; but no society can afford this cheapness, because ultimately it makes every other human activity cheap and shoddy. As time goes on, it degrades the master as well as the slave. It has often been observed that the warders of lunatic asylums gradually become eccentric; and if these posts were hereditary, there can be no doubt that after the lapse of a few generations it would be hard to distinguish between the mental quality of the warders and their charges. In the same way, the existence of slavery, whether it is conducted in a Roman villa, a Japanese cotton mill, or a Whitechapel sweat-shop, is apt to warp the mind of the slave owner.

The most picturesque of the slaves were the gladiators who fought beasts and other men in the arena. Even to-day you can see traces of the arenas where Roman prize-fights were held. You can also see the remains of Roman temples, which were built in great profusion to honour a large number of gods. For instance, there were political temples, because the Roman Emperors, for governmental reasons, made themselves gods by law. There were the ancient gods and goddesses of the Mediterranean world, the goddess of love and the god of wine. There were also the Egyptian gods whose followers believed in immortality. The teaching of Christ came from the East too.

How the Roman Church Began

CHRIST was born in Judea halfway through the reign of the first Roman emperor, who was a nephew of Julius Cæsar. It was then fifty years since Cæsar had landed his troops in Kent.

Christ began to preach during the reign of the second Roman Emperor. His teachings were outrageous to everybody who wanted to preserve existing customs and ways of thinking. He outraged the Jews by suggesting that people of other races were equally entitled to the fatherly love of God. He outraged the priests by laughing at the smugness of formal religion. He outraged all vested interests by teaching that every human being is a living temple of God, and implying that all men are equal in the sight of God. His teaching, in short, conferred a sort of dignity, honour and freedom on every man alive, even the poorest and most degraded; and this was inevitably resented by rich men, priests, politicians, slave-drivers, civil servants and many others who stood to gain by exploiting the weakness and credulity of other men.

At the height of his career, therefore, Christ was arrested and crucified with two minor rebels against the social order. Before he was judicially murdered, he said: 'Everyone that is of the truth heareth my voice.' 'What is truth?' said jesting Pilate, the Roman Governor. As time went on, more and more people found the answer to this question in the teachings of Christ, and within three centuries Christianity had become the official religion of the Roman Empire.

At first the followers of Christ had to face ruthless persecution, under which many of them died. Human life was almost as cheap in the days of the Empire as in 1914. Besides, the Christians refused to reverence the official god, the Emperor; they were thus political criminals as well as religious and social reformers. Yet the Christian Church grew with the growing consolidation of the Empire, much as capitalism grew with the extension of the British Empire. The Church was grounded early in Rome, the imperial capital; and from this centre new communities were rapidly launched in all the cities, under the control of bishops. The effect of persecution was to harden the Christians in their faith, to increase their self-reliance, and to strengthen their power of attraction for the stronger spirits of the time, whose minds were not shut to new impressions and who were only exhilarated by dangerous living.

England Becomes an Outpost of Empire

THE first Roman conquest of England began in the year 43. (Five hundred years later Rome was to conquer the island again, but the invaders then were Roman priests instead of Roman legions.)

There were good reasons for adding England to the Empire. England was rich in crops and minerals, which were not fully exploited. Under her native chiefs, she was a troublesome neighbour to the Roman province of France. If England was annexed, France would be more quiet, and the Empire would have a fresh source of wealth to tap.

The immediate cause of the invasion was the tribal brawls of England. Shakespeare's King Cymbeline, the acknowledged master of many starveling kings, left a number of claimants who fell out among themselves, and some of them tried to get the Romans on their side. The same thing happened in Ireland a thousand years later, when discredited chieftains called in the cunning help of the Anglo-Norman barons and thus began the Anglo-Irish comedy.

Unlike modern civilized nations when they contemplate a murderous attack on a weaker people, the Romans were not obliged to cloak their real motives under humanitarian excuses. The

White Man's Burden was nothing to the Romans. They were recognized masters of military science and civil administration, and like all genuine masters they gloried in the exercise of their craft and saw that they were handsomely paid for it.

The Britons put up a good fight, and the Emperor Claudius himself had to bring reinforcements. He came with a number of elephants, which alarmed the Britons as much as a howitzer would alarm Polynesians.

The elephants were just as effective and not as harmful. Having conquered the south, as far as Leicester, and received submission from the native chiefs, the Emperor called himself Britannicus or 'British Claud' much as we might say 'Chinese Gordon'.

Thereafter the conquest was steadily pushed on in the routine Roman way. The most pugnacious of the British chiefs, Caractacus, who refused to accept the position of a Basuto chief under a protectorate, was driven back on the Welsh hills, defeated and captured. By that time the richest half of England was under Roman rule. When Queen Boadicea of Essex took up arms ten years later, because of the weight of Roman taxation, she was in the position of a refractory Indian Prince; that is to say, she was regarded as a rebel,

The Roman masters worked English mines with slave-labour. To-day many British

and the rising was stamped out with much severity.

In a few years more the Roman governor Agricola, having pacified the Southerners and adjusted taxation more fairly, was leading his troops into the North and smashing the Scots in pitched battles. He saw clearly that the conquest of England alone was not enough; Scotland and Ireland too must be brought into the Empire, or the provincial frontiers would always be exposed to the attacks of these ruffian Celts. There might be no Irish question to-day if Agricola had stayed long enough at Government House. Unfortunately he was recalled to Rome.

When Britons were Slaves

UNDER Agricola and his successors the romanization of the British was rapid. The old tribal organization, in which the chieftain was the law-giver and the leader in battle, gave way to a capitalist military civilization.

The chieftains who remained became country gentlemen in the Roman style. They had fine houses, good food, and Roman clothes. Their sons were given a Latin education, and the more ambitious among them were soon practising rhetoric, for oratory, 'the harlot of the arts', was the highest art of Rome. In the same way, Indian princes to-day are encouraged to send their sons to English public schools in order to learn cricket.

In the old days, land was owned jointly by the clan. Now the Roman system of farming was introduced, by which the arable land of each district was divided into three big fields, each of which was left fallow for one year in every three, while in the other two years it was sown with barley and wheat. Round the fields lay the common, used for hay and pasture. The farm labourers were unfree men of various kinds, the more fortunate of whom were allowed to till strips of land in the fields on their own account, though on certain days they were bound to work with the slaves on the masters' land. More corn was produced than ever before; more tin, lead and iron were mined.

Another sign of Roman influence was the growth of cities at strategic points like Chester and London on the great roads. They were garrison towns and market towns combined, with barracks, colonnaded buildings, market squares and public baths in place of the old log cabins of the Briton hamlets. Our counties and county towns are survivals of the Roman local government divisions.

26

From Agricola's time onwards, Roman temples appeared in the towns, taking the place of the old Druid worship. In the ordinary way, the Romans permitted some latitude in the observance of local religions; like most people, they were prepared to be tolerant so long as toleration did not affect their own safety and comfort. But they decided that the Druid priests had too much political power, and rather than run the risk of a fanatical outbreak, they hunted the medicine men down and exterminated them. The British have some-times been forced to do the same thing in Africa.

'Happy is the Country that has no History'

THERE is something to be said for this proverb when we consider that orthodox political history is in the main a narrative of wars, riots and brawls, with a dash of chicanery in the shape of diplomatic intrigue. England has next to nothing in the way of chronicles during her period as a Roman province. This is partly due to the fact that she was at peace, and partly to the fact that she was a comparatively unimportant possession. Her des-tiny was decided at Rome, just as the destiny of British Crown Colonies is decided at an office in Whitehall.

During the second century after Christ, the Roman army, the true link between Rome and her provinces, underwent some drastic changes. At one time it had been composed mainly of Italian freemen, who left their little farms for a period with the standards; but by this time it had acquired a professional tone, and the amateur soldier was a rarity. The scope of recruitment had altered too; provincials and barbarians like the Britons were being drafted into the ranks of the legions. And whereas the army had once been extremely mobile, its regiments being often re-shuffled, it was now becoming localized in particular provinces.

These developments were dangerous to the unity of the Empire, because henceforward every provincial governor had at his back what amounted to a personal army, implicitly obedient to his commands. The soldiers had no high tradition as citizens; they were mercenaries who welcomed an ambitious general because his advancement meant prize-money and good living for his followers. Thus it is not surprising to find a Roman governor of Britain being proclaimed Emperor towards the end of the second century. He was defeated by the true Emperor Septimius Severus, who died at York. 'I found the Empire in chaos,' he said on his deathbed, 'but I leave it ordered—even in Britain!'

The implication was that Britain, being the most distant of the provinces, was the hardest to administer. It was quite true; thereafter there were several British governors who aspired to the throne, and led their legions on the road to Rome.

How England became Christian

AT first, these military adventures were only temporary breaches of the peace; they did not affect the civilian population at large, and it was only at the frontiers and on the coast that the withdrawal of the troops, even for a short time, was felt as a disaster. When strong government returned, as it always did, its first task was to beat back the Scottish raiders in the north and the Irish and Frisian pirates on the coasts. In the South and Midlands (the most thickly peopled parts of the island) there was a peace which lasted for three hundred years.

It was the existence of this peace that made the spread of Christianity possible. From its headquarters at Rome, the Church planted colonies in one imperial city after another, from Athens to York. Halfway through the second century a British chief called Lucius was converted to the faith. He was a rich landlord and the event caused some stir, just as there would be endless newspaper gossip if a modern millionaire became converted to Bolshevism.

Persecutions of the Christians went on from time to time, but their effect now, by drawing attention to the courage, persistence and good temper of the victims, was only to excite the sympathy of the more spirited pagans. When, at the end of the third century, the Emperor Diocletian launched the last great attack on the Church, it failed because in several provinces the bulk of the people had already become Christians.

The turn of the tide came with the accession of the Emperor Constantine, after whom the city of Constantinople takes its name. He was an Englishman by birth, and had been acclaimed Emperor at York. At the height of his power he became a convert and made Christianity the official religion of the Roman Empire. Only twenty years before, the Christians had been the objects of a savage persecution. Now, at a stroke, their Church had become identified with the Roman civilization which overspread Western Europe from the Levant to the Irish Channel.

Constantine's action was dictated by simple faith; but there was also sound policy in his resolve to buttress the Empire with the moral force of Christianity. He was a century too late. Given time and proper support, the Church might have civilized the barbarians on the German frontier of the Empire, and taught them to appreciate the advantages of European unity and peace under strong government. As it was, the Empire was unable to digest its barbarian neighbours, and the armies too had become barbarian in composition, under litigious commanders who made a dash for the throne at the slightest opportunity. The whole position became the more complicated because Constantine had shifted the capital of the Empire from Rome to his city of Constantinople.

The Romans leave England

It was under these circumstances that Britain was finally cut off from the Empire. Successive governors of the island province became pretenders to the throne and went off to press their claims, draining the troops away. This happened for the last time in the year 410, after which year no more legions came to England and no more tribute was paid. The Britons, with their garrisons and governors gone, found themselves faced with attacks from Scots, Irish, Dutch and Germans. In the same way, if the English withdrew from India to-day, the hill-men from the North would terrorize the mild Hindoo.

Europe was in chaos. The half-civilized troops from the German frontier had taken possession of Rome, France and Spain, the Western parts of the Empire. In the breakdown of central government the savage Huns in their turn came sweeping through the gap, looting, burning and murdering under their leader Attila. (Modern newspaper correspondents, by dint of historical research, have drawn an interesting parallel between the Huns under Attila and the Germans under William II.) Turned back from Rome by the Pope, the Huns were defeated in France. But the authority of the Emperor had ended in the West.

The Empire had given four centuries of peace to Europe before it cracked up in face of the barbarian invasions. Its legacies are with us to-day. France, Italy, Spain and England are children of the Empire. England inherits less of the Roman language than the other three; but we have the Roman system of measurements, Roman writing and Roman ideas of property.

The Church remained as the richest legacy of Rome. In the welter of Western Europe, when the roads decayed and grass grew in the streets, when each little community was cut off from the old central government to fend for itself, the Church kept its unity and strengthened its hold. There was no power in the West to rival the moral power of the Pope of Rome, who had turned back the Huns when armies collapsed. In this stunned world the Church, through its bishops and priests, kept the idea of European unity alive. The Church alone stood for civilization in the midst of cruelty, misery and squalor.

The Thugs from Germany

FOR nearly two hundred years (from 410-597) England was cut off from the rest of civilized Europe. Her native princes and noble families were left to face attacks from the Scots in the north, the Irish in the west, and the seagoing Germans in the east. The regular army had been sucked into the Continental whirlpool, and the princes had to put up a makeshift resistance on their own account. They managed surprisingly well in the circumstances, for it must be remembered that they were civilians with improvised local levies fighting against thugs who lived by the sword and who had all to gain and nothing to lose by a raid on civilized parts.

c

The dismal monkish chroniclers of the time have left accounts of the great British victories over the German invaders, whose special delight was the looting and burning of churches. In spite of these victories, the pirates managed to get a foothold on the East Coast, and the skippers of their boats settled on the land which the British owners had hastily evacuated. Along the Sussex coast, in Kent, in East Anglia, in the East Riding, and in Northumberland, the pirates were masters of the seaboard. The servile labourers on the farms, whose position had begun to improve with the coming of Christianity, found themselves working under a new class of squires and bailiffs. The Low-German jargon, incorporating some Latin and Celtic elements, became the East-English dialect, and a rowdy set of piratical gods ousted Christianity in this long angle of the country.

In all the Midlands and the West Country the Britons kept their language, their Christian religion, their habits of life and thought. But they could not keep the political unity which Roman governors had imposed, because they no longer had the cement of a strong army; and the priesthood, cut off from contact with Rome, dissipated its energy.

In every part of England the strongest man of

each district became its ruler; and because the Roman tradition lingered, they called themselves princes, and the whole country became a dung-hill of wrangling and squalid little kingdoms.

The life of the common man, the labourer bound to the soil, went on with little change. He tilled the soil for his master, whether British or East-Coast German, in the old Roman way. The field that lay fallow this year would bear wheat next year, and barley the year after.

This was the position in England when Pope Gregory the Great, in the year 597, sent the French monk Augustine as a missionary to England.

Pope Gregory and the English Slaves

Two distinct developments in Europe led to Augustine's landing in Kent; and both of them were directly due to the decline of the Emperor's power in the West. One was the growth of the Pope's power. The other was the rise of strong kings in France.

With the Imperial court fixed permanently in Constantinople, the Popes of Rome became the most important supports of the Empire in the West of Europe. Not only did they stand for all that was orderly and efficient in the old order of things; not only were they recognized as the official heads of the Christian religion which was rapidly converting and civilizing the barbarian invaders: they were also, by force of circumstance, the temporal rulers of a great part of Italy. The strongest and most fearless of them all, Gregory the Great, brought the Church to the highest point it had yet known. He commanded the imperial armies in Italy, and made peace there; he systematized the offices of the Church; he actively encouraged the monastic system, and the Benedictine monks who penetrated every country were his spiritual army, his propagandists and henchmen.

Gregory had a firm ally in the new royal family of Paris, which had come to power over most of France during the bad times and troubles. Late in the sixth century, a French princess of this family was married to the descendant of a German skipper who called himself King of Kent. She brought her own bishop to Britain with her and so re-introduced the practice of the Christian religion.

About this time Gregory the Great saw some child-slaves from pagan East England exposed for sale in an Italian market-place. The unpleasant sight gave him the idea of bringing all

England back to Christianity by converting the Eastern pagans and getting into touch with the old Christians of the Midlands and West. When he appointed Augustine as the chief missionary, it was sensible and natural to send him first to Kent, because the Kentish Court had a French-Christian connection. This was the chancy way in which Canterbury became the religious capital of England.

Roman Priests and Irish Monks

'WE needs must love the highest when we see it.' This is not generally true; but it may be applied with justice to 'King' Ethelbert of Kent in his dealings with Augustine the French priest. The whole Kentish court was converted to Christianity in a very short time, and Augustine was free for his main job, which was to bring the old Christians of West England into fresh contact with Rome, from which they had been cut off for two hundred years.

A meeting between Augustine and the seven British bishops was arranged in the Midlands. Augustine was a keen man of affairs, and to him the bishops, after their long seclusion, were little more than local oddities. They clung passionately to their provincial habits; for instance, they were not prepared to bring their church calendar into line with that of Rome. The church re-union ended in a heated quarrel, and Augustine departed uttering prophetical threats.

This was an important quarrel, because it meant that in the future the advance of the Roman church in England would proceed only from the German-speaking East Coast. The Roman church was the only organizing and cultural force of the time; and the natural consequence of its progress from east to west of the country was that it carried the German dialects with it. This is the reason why the English language contains many words of German origin.

At first it was not at all certain that the Roman church would win. It took advantage of inter-marriage between the East-Coast kinglets to push northwards as far as Tyneside. But the kings of Northumberland were disastrously defeated by the Midlanders and the Welsh; and for thirty years afterwards the Christianity of the North Country was dominated by Irish monks, who had much in common with the old Christians of England and Wales. The North might have remained Celtic-speaking and unromanized until to-day—another Ireland—if it had not been for an energetic priest called Wilfred who became Abbot of

Ripon. At a big meeting held in a convent at Whitby, this Wilfred persuaded the King of Northumberland to adopt the Roman church in his court.

This was a decisive moment. The Irish priests retired in dudgeon; and Ireland was not brought into full communion with Rome till five hundred years later. But in England the battle was won for Rome. The next Archbishop of Canterbury was Theodore of Tarsus, a Greek, who very rapidly organized the division of England into bishoprics and introduced the Roman enthusiasm, order and discipline. The parts where paganism lingered were evangelized so speedily as to leave the impression that the pagan gods must have been a very poor lot. As the Church advanced, so did learning and manners, and so did the German dialects. Soon the Celtic language had almost died out in England; only in Wales and Cornwall it lived on. In later times the same thing was to happen in Ireland, when the English language drove the Irish tongue to the West Coast; so that the Sinn Feiners of our own time have had a great task to revive the old dialect, being driven to offer money prizes to those who would learn to speak fluent Irish.

French Charles and English Egbert

As the Church tightened its grip on the island, the English began to realize themselves as one people, instead of a number of small peoples like Yorkshiremen, East Anglians and Northumbrians. The quarrelsome local princes who used to wrangle endlessly among themselves were forced to recognize the authority and power of a supreme English king.

The first supreme king was Offa, a Midlander. The second was Egbert, a Hampshire man, who fixed his headquarters at Winchester. He was the remote ancestor of the present King George V.

Both Offa and Egbert, through the influence of the Church, were in constant touch with affairs on the Continent. Exciting things had been happening in Europe. The Mahommedans had begun a great conquering drive; they had overrun Spain, and for a time it seemed possible that they would become masters of the Western world, with white men as their slaves. At the critical moment Europe gathered herself together to repel the savage attack. Two forces combined to save Europe. One was the moral and political force of the Popes. The other was the strong arm of the French kings, who flung the brown invaders back across the Pyrenees and pushed

40

Christian civilization forward into Germany. This tremendous alliance was cemented in the year 800, when the French King Charles was crowned by the Pope as Emperor of the West.

It was a restoration, under new conditions, of the Roman Empire. It was a symbol of the unity, under Pope and Emperor, of Christian Europe.

The Emperor Charles (commonly called Charles the Great, or Charlemagne) was a terrific figure, a man of inexhaustible energy and boundless faith. He lived in the saddle, and his conquests over the Germans were invariably followed by compulsory conversion to Christianity.

In these heroic times, both Offa and Egbert had close dealings with the Emperor and the Pope. Offa, for instance, was the first English king to institute regular payments to Rome. He also had correspondence with Charles the Great on the subject of English pilgrims to the Holy City; it appeared that some of these devout persons were really commercial travellers who adopted the disguise of pilgrims to avoid the payment of customs duties. These bogus pilgrims were not typical, however, for English and Irish priests were among the most vigorous and successful missionaries to the Germans whom Charles had thrashed.

As for King Egbert, he had passed his ambitious

youth on the staff of Charlemagne, and was full of European ideas. On his own small scale he followed his master's lead, and made himself undisputed overlord of England. He carried his arms even to Land's End, to cow the backwoodsmen of Cornwall. But a shadow fell over the end of his reign. Four years before he died he had to beat back the first big raid of the Danish pirates.

The Big Blond Beasts

THE Danes were the last heathen invaders of England. Since then, we have had incursions of the French and the Dutch; but both of these were civilized Christian types, and their elements were easily assimilated.

The Danes began their piratical voyages because life at home had become intolerable. Charlemagne's progress through Germany had alarmed the heathen of the Baltic. They began to look for a livelihood across the water. When the first bold spirits set off from home in their dragonships and landed in England, they found a wonderful land to loot. There were rich churches and monasteries, the gifts of pious landowners; and there was no mobile army to cope with invaders, because the English kings had to rely on a muster of farmers, and farmers are notorious individualists except at times when the tithe collectors are busy, when they combine with the alacrity of hydrogen and oxygen.

In these circumstances a few boatloads of buccaneers, with no other object than booty, could work havoc in an entire county. They commandeered horses, robbed and burned churches and monasteries, and tortured, mutilated and killed the inmates in a variety of playful ways. Then they were galloping back to the ships before the countryside could be raised in feeble resistance.

The English were stunned. Their first impulse was to buy the pirates off, which they did; but it was only a temporary relief, because the Danes returned with their friends and asked for better terms. At last they began to settle; they spread over the North-Eastern counties (those farthest from the capital at Winchester) and garrisoned the towns. A rough organization grew up between the different pirate crews, as though a hundred Captain Kidds or Al Capones had agreed to band their murderous ruffians together. They surged over the Eastern Counties and began to claw at the Midlands. It seemed as though England would slide back to heathendom and savagery. At this moment King Alfred, commonly called the Great, began the great rally of the English.

43

This death-fight was not primarily a racial matter. It was primarily a struggle between civilized men and savages, with the odds on a savage victory.

Alfred (the Great)

ALFRED was the English Charlemagne. He held England for civilization as Charlemagne had held Northern Europe. Both were terrific fighters, and both were devoted to the Church. But Alfred was much more complex than the heroic and simple emperor. As a child he had been twice to Rome, and the tradition of Rome was part of his life. He was well read, fond of learning, and susceptible to women. All his life he was dogged by bad health. Circumstances made him a man of action and discovered in him an iron will, which triumphed over weak nerves, illness, defeat and disappointment.

He began the fight against the Midland Danes by paying them a levy which afforded a short relief. Seven years later he defeated them in a decisive battle and made a treaty which penned them in the North and East and bound them to become Christians. The second clause was all-important; it meant that civilization had won the day. Alfred had established an army system

44

which worked; he had built ships to meet the Danish long-boats; he now set up a series of forts along the frontier behind which the Danes had settled. Alfred died in the year 900; fifty years later, as a result of his work, his grandson had become King of all England again, conquering the Welsh and defeating the Scots.

Having saved England, Alfred proceeded to reform her. He codified the rude laws of the time. He encouraged learning, and had translations made from Latin into English. He lent all his power to revive the Church, which had been badly damaged during the troubles, but which now, with its old resilience, took possession of the converted Danes who had made their homes in England and were in process of becoming Englishmen. The Church had no rival as a civilizing agent. It throughly digested the Danish immigrants. Unlike the Italian and Irish immigrants in modern America, they were given no chance of becoming gangsters or corrupt political wire-pullers.

How the English Squire got Power

ALTHOUGH the Danes were amalgamated so easily with the English people of the East Coast, their raids had a lasting effect on the social structure of England.

Before the Danes came, the central kingship had been growing more powerful. But in the black days when any country village might find itself suddenly attacked by a wild squadron thundering down to rob and kill and burn, the local landlords and squires became like kings of their own districts, because they were the only people with strong houses and the power of protecting the villagers. Thus in their own little way the squires became judges and masters over their own bit of countryside. The villagers, in return for the squire's protection, became his retainers. They held their land as his tenants, and were bound to work his farm without wages. It is this social system which later historians have called Feudalism.

The poor man's life was better under feudalism than it had been before. To begin with, old forms of slavery were dying out under the influence of the Church. The feudal labourer was bound to the land, and on certain days of the week he had to work on the master's farm; but his own right to the produce of certain strips of land in the three great fields was recognized by his master and everyone else. That is to say, he was a small farmer on his own account, as well as being a labourer on his master's account. He might be called a serf; but in practice he was more free than the average labourer of to-day. Most of the unemployed miners in South Wales would gladly exchange economic positions with the feudal labourer of the tenth century.

The Danish wars and the growth of feudalism had a damaging effect on the discipline of the Church. In some districts which had become more and more isolated, the priests got married and became family men. Many other priests kept mistresses more or less openly. And in the higher places of the Church there was much sordid bargaining and scrambling for the wealthier jobs. The clergy would have lost a great deal of their prestige if St. Dunstan had not come on the scene at the critical moment.

Saint Dunstan and the Parsons

HE was a gay West-Country squire, with a taste for learning and a love of tunes, inspired by the Irish priests who taught him. Good birth, good manners, and masterful ways accounted for his rapid progress in the Church. At the age of nineteen he was Abbot of Glastonbury, and afterwards he became in turn Bishop of Worcester, Bishop of London, and Archbishop of Canterbury.

47

Dunstan was a power in the land for nearly forty years, as the right-hand man of several young kings who inherited Alfred's bad health. He was exiled once, by a vicious lad who held the crown for a year or two; but he came back stronger than ever, and being an older, firmer, and quicker man, was able to keep the next kings in leading-strings. This was a good thing for the country, because he kept it at peace.

It was a good thing for the Church, too. Dunstan proceeded to reform it according to the principles laid down at the French abbey of Cluny, which at that time was leading the battle against slack clergymen. Dunstan's method of restoring discipline was to revive the monasteries, to eject married priests, and to eliminate jobbery among toadies and tuft-hunters who aimed at bishoprics. Unfortunately this work was largely undone by a new outbreak of the Danish wars.

Shall England be Danish or French?

THE first stroke of the new Danish brawls came after Dunstan's death, when Ethelred the Unready was king.

By this time the Danes had become Christians. From being savages, they had become civilized men. This took the edge off their brutality, but increased their strength, because English malcontents and criminals no longer hesitated to join forces with the invaders.

The wretched Ethelred took two measures to strengthen his hand. First, he married a Norman princess named Emma. Normandy at that time was the strongest and best-ruled state in all Europe.

Secondly, Ethelred ordered a cold-blooded massacre of all the Danes recently settled in England. This was on St. Brice's Day, in the year 1002. The order was carried out with admirable thoroughness. Seldom has a king seen such gratifying obedience to his wishes. The Danes and their wives were butchered.

The effects of this policy were disastrous. Whole fleets put out from Denmark and Norway in an unchristian spirit of revenge. Year after year they swept down on England, burning and plundering, until at last Ethelred fled to his brother-in-law in Normandy, and the Danish Canute became King of England.

Canute was half Dane, half Pole, and wholly Catholic. He married Ethelred's Norman widow. He kept a strong peace in England, which was only a fraction of his great Northern empire. The true note of his reign is his pilgrimage to Rome.

He steadily supported the Church as the agent of peace, order, and civilization. When he died, England had had twenty years of strong government and was ready for more.

Canute's oafish and short-lived sons were succeeded by King Edward the Confessor, a fat, simple and pious albino, the son of Ethelred the Unready and Emma of Normandy. He had been brought up as a Frenchman, and he imported Normans to rule for him. While he lived there was a struggle for supremacy between these Norman immigrants and the great earls of England. When he died, in 1066, the issue lay between William of Normandy (Edward's cousin) and Harold, Earl of Wessex (Edward's brother-in-law). Harold has been called the Last of the Saxons; he might just as sensibly be called the Last of the Danes, for his mother was Danish. Harold had the advantage of being on the spot. Having proclaimed himself king, he had to smash a rebellion by his precious brother in the North. He then marched with tired troops to meet William of Normandy at Hastings. He was killed, and his army was hopelessly defeated. This was the beginning of the Norman Conquest.

E ngland was Catholic for a thousand years. The Church prevented profiteering and unscrupulous finance, cared for the old and unemployed, ran universities, schools and hospitals. It provided a complete system for the social, economic and intellectual life of the nation

Simple Faith and Norman Blood

THE Norman conquerors were strong supporters of the Pope and the Church. There is a well-known poem by Kingsley which says:

> *'Kind hearts are more than coronets*
> *And simple faith than Norman blood.'*

The first line may be true; but the second draws a false distinction. In 1066 Norman blood was actually a guarantee of simple faith; and wherever the Normans went they strengthened the Church.

The Church in those days was the cement that held Europe together. In fact, Europe was properly called Christendom: the land of Christian men. The only true patriotism of the time was Christianity. The only patriotic wars were the Crusades, waged by all the peoples of Europe (including the English) against the Mahommedans. The unexpressed motto of the Crusades was 'Christendom for the Christians'. The Crusades were launched and kept alive by the Church.

The Church was the greatest social force in the world. Every man in Christendom, from the labourer to the king, was a member of the

51

Church. From his baptism to his death he was daily aware of its influence. It touched life at every point—family life, politics, business and pleasure. An outcast from the Church was a social outcast too, regarded by his neighbours as a moral leper, like a boycotted man in the Ireland of Parnell.

The Church monopolized thought and learning, literature and science. It set up schools and universities. It encouraged the arts. Its buildings were (and are) glorious. It offered a career open to talent. The poor man with ambition, the rich man with public spirit; the scholar, the administrator, the mystic, the lawyer—all gravitated towards the Church.

And with all this wealth of brains and energy, the Church impressed its teachings on the life of the community. For instance, it forbade usury, the system by which debenture holders and moneylenders prey on modern communities. Again, the Christian system allowed merchants and manufacturers to fix a 'just price' for their goods, but not to make an excessive profit—a code which, if applied to-day, would disqualify advertising quacks and many other parasitic traders.

In maintaining its influence, the Church had the great advantage of discipline. Every normal man recognized the moral authority of his parish priest. The priest was directly responsible to his bishop. Over all was the unquestioned authority of the Pope.

A Church, like a Government, must be paid for. In those days the Church was paid in land and labour. For instance, the parish priest was often a small farmer, with strips of land in the common fields. The bishop, in his turn, was a big landowner—a squire or lord of the manor. At that time the ownership of English land carried duties as well as privileges—the duty of supervising local government, and the duty of supplying soldiers in time of need for the service of the universal overlord, the king. Thus the bishop was simultaneously a royal official and a church official, a king's officer and a pope's officer. Both the Pope and the king had an interest in the method of appointing and controlling bishops; and when Pope and king differed, the results were disastrous.

Pope's Men and King's Men

FOR a long time after 1066 both the Pope of Rome and the King of England were fully occupied, and there was no hint of tension between them.

William the Conqueror's first task as king was to reward his French followers with gifts of English land. He used much discrimination in sharing the spoils, because he was quite determined not to have any landowner as powerful as the late Harold's family had been. As a further brake on the barons, William set up a rough civil service of sheriffs to watch his interests locally. At the same time the wealth and customs of England were systematically surveyed, much as a modern advertising agent might survey the English market to find the buyers for his goods. Domesday Book shows that the duties, possessions and position of every man in England were defined with a precision worthy of a rapacious tax collector.

The Conqueror was too grimly efficient to rouse the enthusiasm of his English subjects. They called him William the Bastard, but not abusively, for he was in fact illegitimate; and though they did not like him or his friends personally, they appreciated the law and order which he enforced.

William's greatest contemporary, the Pope Gregory VII, roused both enthusiasm and hatred. Gregory was a man of mean appearance and origin, who had started life as a monk under the name of Hildebrand. He burned to see the Church free of all secular interference, staffed only by able, sincere and loyal men, and powerful enough to control the dangerous fancies and mischievous quarrels of kings, so that everybody might grow more perfect in a peaceful and united Christendom.

Thus as soon as Gregory came to power he purged the Church by casting out married priests and forbidding kings to appoint bishops. The second ordinance, for reasons already given, put him at odds with the Emperor of Germany, the most powerful ruler in Europe, who felt that he could not afford to lose the right of appointing such great officers as bishops. But the Pope's authority was stronger than the emperor's wealth and troopers; and the Emperor, with his subjects in open rebellion, at last stood barefoot in the snow outside the castle of Canossa, begging for absolution from the Pope.

No English king figured in such a dramatic scene; but the Conqueror's son, Henry I, had a quarrel on the same subject with the Archbishop of Canterbury, Anselm. Henry was a tactful man, and agreed to a compromise by which bishops were freely elected by the cathedral clergy, but in the presence of the king; and after election they had to do homage to the king for their estates. This seemed a sensible solution: the bishops were appointed for their record of service in the

Church, but formally recognized that as great landholders they had certain duties to perform for the king.

King Henry and Saint Thomas of Canterbury

BETWEEN the death of Henry I and the accession of Henry II, a benevolent nonentity called Stephen was King of England. Hell is paved with benevolence; and England during Stephen's reign was a hell upon earth, with the great landowners busily engaged in cutting each others' throats. There was no security for life and property, and everyone except the wealthy brawler was glad when the ruthless Henry II took Stephen's place.

There was nothing benevolent about Henry II. He had a villainous temper and the energy of a demon. He was as hard as nails and had an iron grip on facts. He would have agreed with Napoleon that 'only the weakling is evil'. In short, he was a good king because he was strong enough to keep the peace.

England was not Henry's only possession. He owned lands in France, from Normandy to the Spanish borders. Among his subjects were the southern knights who held courts of love in honour of their ladies, and troubadours with their lutes and ballads, and comedians who tramped the roads, and jolly masons who built the lovely churches. Soon a great part of Ireland was added to Henry's property, when the Irish kings fell out among themselves and one of them got help from the Anglo-Norman knights. The Pope gave his blessing to the Norman conquest of Ireland, as he had given his blessing to the Norman conquest of England. He wanted to grip the Irish clergy in the discipline of Rome, and he succeeded.

Yet Henry II, like his forerunners, had a brush with the Church and came off worst. Like all kings at the time, he had to employ a priest to control his civil service, since priests were the only educated men who could be got for the job. He managed to pick an able and resolute man called Thomas Becket, who performed with such ability that Henry was glad to have him made Archbishop of Canterbury. It proved an unlucky move for Henry. Becket had a high notion of the duties of his new office, and instead of remaining a catspaw of the king, he upheld the rights of the Church with fierce zeal. Henry resented the change in his favourite, whom he regarded as a turncoat and denounced with great bitterness, so that in the upshot a gang of toadying rascals, hot from an audience with the king, murdered the Archbishop in his own cathedral. All England was aghast at the crime. The victim became Saint Thomas of Canterbury, and pilgrims flocked to his shrine. Henry made peace with the Church and did public penance at Canterbury. Public opinion forced him to do it. The Church was more powerful than the king.

Why Englishmen fought in Palestine

HENRY II's son Richard (called 'The Lionheart') was the first King of England to go Crusading.

The Crusades were the wars fought by the united Christians of Europe against the advancing Asiatics. The wars began with a successful Christian attempt to dislodge the Turks from the holy city of Jerusalem, where a Christian kingdom was set up. French, Italians, Dutch, Germans, English and even Scots took part in this first great campaign. 'The Frenchman forsook his hunting, and the Scot forsook his fleas.'

The new kingdom of Jerusalem had to maintain itself in the teeth of incessant attacks, and needed constant supplies of men from Europe. In 1187 the great Emir Saladin recaptured Jerusalem for the Saracens, and the kingdom was reduced to a few coast towns. This second fall of Jerusalem was the signal for a new Crusade, led by Philip of France and Richard of England.

A soldier by calling, a Christian by conviction, an adventurer by instinct, Richard revelled in the idea of conducting a holy war. He was the most popular man in Europe. Everyone sympathized with his aims, everyone admired his reckless courage, his indomitable energy, his lavish generosity. A king who exceeds his professional duties by becoming a hero is an expensive luxury for his subjects. Richard was expensive. He squeezed England of fighting men, sailors, money and ships, to fit up the great expedition. Yet the cause and its leader had such a grip on the imagination of the English that the money was not grudged and there was an enthusiastic muster to the flag.

The Crusade was not successful, because of quarrels between the followers of the French and English kings. Richard recaptured the city of Acre, but in face of the treachery of Philip of France he failed before Jerusalem, which remained in the hands of the Saracens. On his return from the Holy Land, Richard was kidnapped in Germany and had to be ransomed with English gold. He had failed in the greatest adventure of his life, but he had carried himself so well that he became a legend of courage even to the Saracens, and a source of pride to Englishmen.

59

It was ironical that this Crusade—a gesture of united Europe—should be defeated by internal dissensions among the Christian armies. Yet for many years afterwards there was a flow of adventurers from England to the Holy Land, and another King of England, Edward I, was fighting the battles of Christendom at Acre a hundred years after Richard had regained the city with his English troops.

Magna Carta gave Liberty to Millionaires

WHILE Richard was fighting abroad, England was well governed by priests. When the Christian hero died, he was succeeded by his brother John, a self-indulgent rascal who united a quarrelsome disposition and offensive manners with a stupid and cowardly character. He soon succeeded in making himself loathed by every respectable element in the community.

His first exploit was to lose all the family possessions in France except Gascony and to irritate all the great landowners by various money-raising expedients. His second folly was to try fleecing the Church at a time when a clever and resourceful Pope was in power. He paid for both imbecilities by two great surrenders.

The first surrender was the signing of Magna Carta, the 'great' charter. It was forced on him by a combination of armed landowners, townsmen and priests. The Charter, regarded as a blow for liberty, is not in itself an impressive document. It merely defined the rights of landowners, traders, and other wealthy classes. The farm workers, who constituted nine-tenths of the population, were hardly mentioned. If they heard of the Charter at all, their attitude would have resembled that of an unemployed modern labourer confronted with an impassioned manifesto by millionaires, screen actresses, and racehorse owners against the evils of income tax and death duties.

The importance of the Charter was that it set the Law above the exactions of good kings and bad kings alike, and so secured the interests of all people who had wealth and position. In future, whenever the landowners had a grievance against the king, they could quote the definitions of the Charter to justify themselves.

John's second surrender was to the power of the Church. His stupid policy of plundering the wealth of the English Church led to his excommunication. This was serious enough to a private individual, because it meant ostracism and boycotting; but it was disastrous to the king, because his subjects were released from their duty to him, and could be treasonable and seditious with a clear conscience. The Church broke John, and only pardoned him on condition that he recognized in the Pope the temporal as well as the spiritual overlord of England. John accepted the condition. He had no alternative. It was the Church's day of power.

The Pope could do with English Money

WHEN John's life guttered out, and he was succeeded by his son Henry III, the Popes were beginning the last phase of their long quarrel with the Holy Roman emperors who reigned over Germany and Italy. The quarrel had begun because of the dual position of the bishops as royal officers and papal officers at the same time; it continued because of disputes about Italian lands which were claimed by both Pope and Emperor, and because the Popes, in the interest of peace and humanity, made perpetual attempts to control the wanton caprice of all bad rulers, among whom John of England was a dreadful example.

As far as England was concerned, the main result of the Pope's troubles was a constant drain of money to Rome. Henry III, a pious man with very little sense, enforced the Pope's demands. As an inadequate reward for his loyalty, the empty titles of King of the Romans and King of Sicily were bestowed on his brother and his second son respectively. Even in those days titles could be bought. There are sound precedents for the war profiteers of 1918 who became lords by subscribing to party funds.

The English landowners, who believed that one king in the royal family was quite enough, were incensed at Henry's policy of supporting the Pope's exactions. It caused them great pain to see good money flowing away from England. They were also jealous of the foreigners who swarmed at Court and fattened on the king's generosity. They complained that Henry had infringed the definitions of the 'great' Charter which John's ineptitude had made possible.

At last they began to organize another rebellion. Their leader was Simon de Montfort, himself a Frenchman who had been a favourite at Court, a man of the world who had fought in a recent Crusade. He defeated the king at Lewes and then called the first English Parliament. This was a pure experiment. In justice to de Montfort, it must be said that he could not foresee the results of his action.

63

The First English Parliament

THE word 'parliament' simply means 'talking'. Since Alfred's times there had always been a national talking club, composed of the big landowners and called together when the king wanted their advice. This was the origin of the House of Lords.

De Montfort's experiment was to call a House of Commons as well—two squires from each county and two local magnates from each town. He called them together because he wanted to get support for himself from the smaller landowners and the merchants as well as from the big landowners who sided with him. Just as a Trade Union Congress to-day is held with the object of devising plans for squeezing the capitalists, de Montfort's Parliament was a party gathering for curtailing the king's liberty.

The king's cause, however, had a quick revival. About a year after the battle at Lewes, Henry's eldest son Edward smashed de Montfort's men at Evesham. This Edward was soon to be King of England and he perpetuated de Montfort's experiment in Parliament-making.

Unpopularity of Early Members of Parliament

EDWARD I certainly had no intention of posing for posterity as a reformer. He would have re-volved in the grave if he could have seen how Parliament would develop under the leadership of men like Lloyd George and Ramsay Mac-Donald. He was in fact strictly a man of his time. He fought lustily on his crusade in Palestine; he conquered the Welsh, hammered the Scots, and bickered with the French. To his lasting surprise, all three nations resented his activities; and in 1295, when he was confronted with rebellion in Wales and Scotland and war in France, he called together the alleged 'model' Parliament on the same lines as de Montfort's. It was only from Edward's point of view that the Parliament was a model. He called it together to explain that money was needed for carrying on three wars, and it was clearly understood that the Parliament had to see that this money was handed over to the king's tax collectors. Nobody wanted to belong to such a Parliament. An M.P. in those days was merely an unpopular man with bad news, and some gentlemen fled the country when they heard that they had been elected. It was only in later days, under weaker kings than Edward, that the M.P.s began to see possibilities

E

in their position. If the king needed money badly enough they could haggle with him and extort privileges for themselves! But this did not occur to them for a long time. So Edward got his money and continued to fight. He crushed the Welsh and wedded Wales to England, becoming thus indirectly responsible for the later exploitation of South Welsh coalfields and North Welsh seaside resorts, as well as for the emotional religious revivals which took the place of frustrated political ambition. But he failed to hold the calculating Scots, who in this reign began their long and troublesome alliance with the French. Scotland and France screwed themselves on either side of England like nutcrackers, but England under a hard-fighting, hard-taxing king was too tough a nut for them.

How the Church fell on Bad Times

EDWARD's enthusiasm for gathering taxes led him into a pretty quarrel with the Church. The contemporary Pope was Boniface VIII, who prescribed that no taxes should be laid on the clergy without the Pope's sanction. Archbishop Winchelsey of England supported the Pope's attitude against the king. Edward was a man of strong likes and dislikes. The chief of his dislikes were tax-dodgers and Jews. In these circumstances both the Archbishop and the Jews were deported from England.

This was not the worst defeat which Pope Boniface received. He quarrelled with Philip of France, a much less respectable and scrupulous man than Edward. Philip worked on his criminal associates to seize the Pope and throw him into prison after dragging him through the streets tied backwards on an ass.

Boniface died under this course of treatment, and for seventy years after his death the Popes were in the power of the French kings, holding their capital at Avignon instead of Rome. This was a tragedy for Europe. For hundreds of years the Popes had fought to keep themselves free of political bias. They knew that their power rested ultimately in the faith of simple folk, and to keep that power they must be independent of kings and rich men with private axes to grind. Thus on countless occasions they faced poverty, exile and death rather than compromise with those whose policy would have broken the Christian unity of Europe. Yet now, after all these fierce struggles and noble sacrifices, the Popes had become 'captives in Avignon', tools of the French kings, and the Papacy itself had become a French institution.

The immediate effects were disastrous. If a strong Pope had been in power, the long wars between the French and English kings might have been cut short. As it was, the captive Popes were allies of the French kings, lending them large sums of money as well as moral support. In spite of this scandal, the Church maintained its power in the daily life of town and village. Its socially beneficent work continued without a break. It remained the pivot of all civil activities. It dictated the rules of honest business, relieved the poor and the sick, founded universities, hostels and schools, taught the arts, built glorious churches and abbeys. It synthesized the spiritual, the intellectual and the social sides of man's life. At the end of the Avignon captivity, England was solidly Catholic still.

Chaucer's England and Ours

IT is true that during this time of papal obscurity a Leicestershire parson named Wycliffe began an agitation against Church abuses and started a sect called the Lollards. But the Lollards were never popular, and Wycliffe's ideas were only supported by the big landowners who itched to get their hands on the Church's money. Rich men's thefts can often be passed off as examples of enterprise and keen business instinct. Thus a tramp who rifles a poor-box is universally condemned, while the mediæval barons who proposed to rob the Church on a really big scale, under cover of Wycliffe's agitation, are regarded by Liberal historians as far-seeing patriots.

The poet Chaucer, a contemporary of Parson Wycliffe, has left us a humorous picture of the time. Some of the priests in Chaucer's funny stories are certainly no angels; but then an author whose chief talent is for comic anecdotes can make very little play with angels or saints. Even so, Chaucer has a memorable description of a poor parson, typical of the time, who devotes every ounce of energy to the work of his parish. It is worth noting, too, that the stories in Chaucer's book are supposed to be told by a band of pilgrims on the road to Canterbury. A modern author who tries to assemble characters of all types and classes into one book is driven to deal with the individual lives of guests in a mammoth hotel or passengers on a liner. But Chaucer found all the characters he wanted in a company of English pilgrims: the crusading knight and the gay young squire, the saintly prioress and the lusty wife, the red-nosed miller and the rapacious bailiff, the Cambridge scholar and the poor parson, the jolly monk and the prosperous farmer. They ride to Canterbury in April weather, all bound to do honour to the English Saint Thomas for the good of their souls, and determined to be merry and agreeable on the way. There is nothing like this in England today. Try to imagine the modern prototypes of Chaucer's men and women lumped together in a big railway carriage: a brass-hat general, a Guards lieutenant, a charity-worker, a grocer's widow, a bookmaker, a works manager, a technical student, an impoverished vicar, a dissenting minister and a dairyman. Their conversation, if recorded, would raise few laughs. For a happy mingling of types and classes, the only modern approximation to Chaucer's pilgrims is the crowd at an Irish race meeting.

The First Scottish Nationalists

IT was while the Popes were wealthy 'captives' in France that the Hundred Years' War between the French and English kings began. Edward I's attempts to make the Scots knuckle under, led to the revolt of Wallace and Bruce, the first Scottish Nationalists, and to an offensive alliance between Scotland and France. Thus while the English kings were leading their armies north of the border, the Frenchmen prepared to lay waste the English possessions in France.

The militant Scots, once roused, found that it was more profitable to unite in raids on England than to cut each other's throats. Edward II was a weak and silly young man who hated trouble; but his father had left him a legacy of Scottish ill-will and he was forced to cross the Tweed with his army. The result was the Scottish victory at Bannockburn.

Edward III, in his turn, had to try a fall with Scotland. He welcomed it, for he thirsted for glory. His head was full of fine women and chivalrous battles, and when he found that Scotland must be fought in France, he was glad of the excuse to pit his English longbowmen and armoured knights against the Frenchmen, at that time reputed the best soldiers in Europe.

Superiority of Mediæval to Modern Wars

'PATRIOTISM is the last refuge of a scoundrel.' It has certainly been the excuse for a great deal of self-indulgence and romantic play-acting. Edward III was our first Patriot King, the first to believe and to make others believe that a genuine love of England was a valid excuse for injuring other peoples. The fighting kings of the past, like Richard I and Edward I, were European rather than English in the accent of their minds. Their idea of glory was to fight for Christian Europe against the Turks, not for themselves against the French.

All blood-sports have their evil side, and there is little doubt that the Hundred Years' War did some harm in the long run both to England and to France. Civilized modern men, however, who associate war with marvels of science like torpedoes, bombs, sixteen-inch shells and poison gas, may be pardoned for regarding the Franco-English skirmishes of the fourteenth century as mere child's play. It is true that a number of towns were burned, a number of women criminally assaulted, a number of civilians killed in cold blood, but it was all done on a small scale. The most lethal weapon in use was the longbow, which in the hands of English yeomen led to the victories of Crécy and Poitiers. The battles were conducted in a gentlemanly fashion, and it was more profitable to take an enemy alive than dead, because a rich prisoner could be traded for a heavy ransom. Thus the war not only provided the young gentry with a manly open-air sport, but appealed to their gambling instincts. Their addiction to the battlefield is hardly to be wondered at when it is remembered that the 'idle' rich of to-day, in their desperate flight from boredom, are prepared to hunt big game, climb Mount Everest, conduct Arctic expeditions, race motor cars and fly over continents.

As the war went on, professional leaders began to appear, and men like the Black Prince of England had to work hard at the business of soldiering in order to maintain their prestige against talented outsiders like the Gascon mercenary du Guesclin. In war, as in cricket, the professional is generally the better man at the job; he cannot afford to play to the gallery, or to take time off at other diversions. In competition with the professionals, the Black Prince became a great soldier, but his sympathies and ideas were too narrow to let him develop into a great man.

How the Farm Labourers got Wages

WHILE the Black Prince was conquering France, the Black Death conquered England. It was a horrible contagious disease which de-populated the countryside and made agricultural labour scarce. For hundreds of years the land system in England had been the same. Most of the labourers tilled their own strips of land in the three big common fields of the village, and instead of paying rent they worked on the squire's land on certain days of the week. There was, however, a small class of so-called 'free' labourers who were paid in money instead of land when they worked for the squire. When the Black Death created a shortage of workers, the 'free' labourers began to demand higher wages, and the others began to see some advantages in being paid in money instead of in land. A great number of them left the ancestral villages and trudged away to hire themselves out to new masters, getting a money wage instead of a bit of land.

Matters adjusted themselves in the end. The farm workers who stuck to their strips of land—the majority—were allowed to pay the rent in cash instead of in work, and were guaranteed by custom in the possession of their land. Many landlords used the rents to pay shepherds and to stock the land with sheep. England was becoming a cloth-making country, and there was a good market for wool. Besides, the landlords found that a successful sheep-run needs less labour than grain-farming. So popular did sheep farming become that before long some of the 'free' labourers were out of work. Their freedom meant freedom to starve. Fortunately the towns, with their growing cloth business, were able to absorb numbers of ex-ploughmen. Otherwise they would have been in the position of the modern coal miner who is thrown out of his job by the growing use of foreign oil.

Of course this revolution in English life did not happen overnight. When the Black Death first dislocated the farming system, many landlords worked themselves into a panic; and as Parliament was manned exclusively by landlords, they managed to pass laws enabling them to compel labourers to do more work and to keep wages down. It was another matter to enforce these laws as long as labour was scarce and an ill-used farm-hand could flit in the night and be welcomed as a tenant by a neighbouring bailiff who was short of hands and asked no questions. Yet the very attempt to put the laws into practice caused bad blood, and when a new tax was levied to meet the expenses of the French war the workmen felt that the limit of human endurance had been reached. In 1381, led by a priest named John Ball and a footpad named Wat Tyler, the labourers of Kent and Essex marched on London, murdered the Archbishop of Canterbury, and burnt the Savoy. Their slogan ran:

'When Adam delved and Eve span,
Who was then the gentleman?'

The contemporary gentlemen and ladies resented the invitation to become diggers and spinners. The boy king, Richard II, saved the situation with great courage by tackling the mob alone and dispersing them with fair promises. These promises were not kept; the labour leaders were afterwards tracked down and killed.

Richard was an intelligent, courageous and charming man, but he was also a creature of moods and fancies. His difficulties were multiplied by the results of the late King Edward's policy, which had been to marry the members of the royal family to scions of the English nobility. This brought into being a powerful class of semi-royal people who manipulated the feeble Parliament against Richard. He was finally deposed by his relative Henry of Lancaster, afterwards known as Henry IV. This cool and self-seeking opportunist, conscious that his title to the throne was not strong, tried to make it seem legal by accepting the crown from Parliament. This was a bad business, because Parliament was composed of landlords who were far better at interfering with the government than directing it. They did not represent the people; they only represented themselves. They could hamper a strong king and ruin a weak one. They hampered Henry V and ruined Henry VI.

Henry the Fifth and Joan of Arc

HENRY THE FIFTH, Shakespeare's hero-king, was a hard and calculating man who pulled himself together after a profligate youth, and became a fanatical churchman. He revived the French war as the best means of diverting the mischievous energy of the great landowners and possibly of killing a few of them off. Thus he probably spoke with deep feeling when he said:

> 'Once more unto the breach, dear friends, once more;
> Or close the wall up with our English dead!'

It happened that France was in a chaotic state, and Henry after a sweeping victory at Agincourt managed to get himself recognized as heir to the French throne. But he died before the union of the crowns could become a permanent arrangement; and what was worse, his heir was an infant in arms. This unfortunate child was Henry VI, the catspaw of the landowners who controlled Parliament.

The first result was that the conquests in France began to fall away. The inspired country girl Joan of Arc put fresh spirit into the French troops, and though the English captured her and she was condemned as a heretic, the tide of victory had turned against the English. Gunpowder and artillery ended the supremacy of the longbow.

Ex-soldiers coming back to England took service with the great landowners, who began to form small private armies, an outrage which no strong king would have tolerated. Unfortunately Henry VI had fits of insanity, and was not very lucid or decisive in his sane intervals. As the Parliament was in the hands of the landowners, there was no redress for the grievances of the nation, who were terrorized by the hired bullies of the squires, and could get no justice in the courts of law. The juries were bribed or intimidated. The royal officers and civil service practically ceased to function. Murder and robbery went unpunished. When the Duke of York, emboldened by Henry's imbecility, put in a claim for the throne, the armed landowners joyfully took sides, and began the Wars of the Roses.

The Wars of the Roses

THIS squalid civil war hardly deserves its flowery name, which derives from the fact that the Duke of York's followers took a white rose as their badge, while Henry's men sported red roses.

The Yorkists had the better of the long and

tedious brawl. Their leader drove out Henry VI and himself became King Edward IV. He was a first-rate soldier, but a gross liver, an assiduous seducer of women, and a treacherous friend. He was exiled once, but celebrated his romantic return by the murder of his demented rival Henry. He then engaged in a fresh war with France, but was soon persuaded to desert his allies and accept a heavy pension from the French king. This is an example of realism in foreign policy. Edward might have said, with a well-known modern financier, 'Nothing is lost save honour'.

His domestic policy showed the same triumph of sense over sentiment. He maintained an army of spies and agents-provocateurs to report cases of sedition, and beheaded offenders with a magnificent disregard for the trivial processes of justice. His earnest desire to make the throne secure and powerful was stronger even than the claims of family affection. He drowned his jealous brother Clarence in a butt of Malmsey wine, a truly royal death.

When Edward died he left two sons, one of whom became Edward V, and a brother, who became Richard III by the drastic method of murdering his two nephews. Edward IV had been a tall, florid and handsome man; Richard was dwarfish, hunchbacked, venomous and clever.

Edward was a gay and debonair murderer whose high spirits and vulgar vices endeared him to the populace; but Richard was too sinister and calculating a criminal to command the affection of his subjects. Students of the history of Chicago's gunmen could doubtless adduce similar cases where one gang-leader's charm has won all hearts while a less attractive ruffian, in spite of superior ability, has met a premature end with a machine-gun bullet. It was so with Richard. Disloyal people put up another claimant to the throne, who killed Richard at Bosworth field and was crowned as Henry VII. This was Henry Tudor, father of bluff King Hal, father-in-law of six queens of England, and grandfather of Queen Mary and Queen Elizabeth.

The Wars of the Roses had not been fought in vain. Its battles were between the professional private armies of great landowners and they resulted in the extinction of a great number of titled brawlers and ne'er-do-wells, with their following of cut-throats, highwaymen and unemployables. The majority of the people had taken no part in the dirty affair. Even at its height, the English towns and trades were growing more prosperous. They only needed strong government to flourish. Nobody cared a brass farthing about Parliamentary liberties. Every respectable person wanted a strong king with an iron hand. That was why Henry Tudor, in many ways an unattractive man, was welcomed to the throne.

When England won her proudest Bays

THE Tudor family gave strong government to England for over a hundred years, from 1485 to 1603. During this time the whole aspect of the world was changed.

America was discovered and England became a sea-power as the Atlantic began to overshadow the Mediterranean in importance. The privateersman Sir Francis Drake circumnavigated the globe. Sir John Hawkins discovered the slave trade as a road to wealth. Sir Walter Raleigh became the first Conquistador of the British Empire, the forerunner of Clive, Wolfe, Raffles, Rhodes and many more.

Raleigh was courtier, historian and poet, in an age of courtiers and poets. This was the time of Spenser, of Jonson, of Marlowe and of Shakespeare, the adventurers in words who now began to exploit the riches of the English tongue as the Spaniards exploited the silver mines of America. The new invention of printing made their works known to everyone who could read.

Poetry flourishes when times are good. England has never been richer than she was in Tudor times, if the wealth of a country is to be judged in the intelligence and well-being of its common men, and not in the vast fortunes of a few financiers and their sycophants. Most of the people got their living from the land, tilling their own acres in the three big fields of the village. For those who had no land there were openings in the market towns, in the fishing fleets, and in the privateers, slave vessels and transatlantic traders.

Yet it was in this Tudor century that England was wrenched out of the direct line of its development, because in this century came the sudden unexpected break with Rome and the gradual break with the European tradition. The consequences were tremendous in every part of English life—in business, in farming, in culture, in politics at home and abroad. No one at the time could visualize these consequences, least of all the booby who brought the change about. Henry VIII, the man who tried to concentrate all power, religious and civil, in the hands of the king, was in the long run responsible for the decay of the Church and the ruin of the monarchy.

The English Reformation an Accident

HENRY VIII's strong position when he came to the throne was due to his father, a skinflint and martinet who strengthened the monarchy by amassing a fortune and setting up the Court of Star Chamber, which cut out the danger of corrupt or intimidated juries.

Young Henry (Bluff King Hal) was determined to cut a fine figure in the world, and he had a competent bear-leader in Cardinal Wolsey, a born stage-manager. There were two other young kings at the time: Francis I of France, a long-nosed young sinner with some talent as a gunner, and Charles V of Spain and the Netherlands, a brilliant light-cavalry leader. When the throne of the Holy Roman Empire fell vacant, all three young fellows threw their money about among the electors to get the title for themselves. Charles, the most conscientious of the three, won an empty victory. He found himself at odds with both his rivals, and with two frightful problems to face: the renewed menace of the Turks under Soliman the Magnificent, and the Protestant movement inspired by Luther in Germany. This movement was primarily a savage criticism of the organization of the Catholic Church, and not of its doctrine.

83

In England also there was strong criticism of certain Church abuses, and many ambitious men turned a jealous eye on the Church's wealth and the Church's hold on high official positions in the Government. But there was very little genuine Protestant feeling, and King Henry was doing a popular thing when he wrote a book against heresy and earned the title Defender of the Faith.

Unfortunately Henry presently began to seek a divorce from his wife Katharine of Aragon, a divorce which only the Pope could grant. The Pope refused. Bluff King Hal was a bluffer, and thought that a display of temper would make the Pope change his mind. In 1529 he turned to his servile Parliament to pass laws against the appointment of English clergy from Rome. Three years later the payment of taxation to Rome was cut off. Within seven years all ties with Rome, legal, financial and judicial, were broken off, and the king assumed the position of an English Pope, being recognized by English law as the 'Supreme Head in earth of the Church of England'.

This mighty change—the result of Henry's infatuation for a lady whom he afterwards beheaded on a charge of adultery—was accompanied by a terrific confiscation of Church property. The monasteries were examined by the king's commissioners, found corrupt, and turned over to the State. Their vast wealth was poured into the pockets of the king's supporters in Parliament, who become millionaires overnight. Some part of the confiscated money was restored to the Church to form new and poorly paid bishoprics. In the same way some modern financiers try to salve their consciences by the establishment of free libraries, university colleges and hospitals.

Unexpected Results of the 'Reformation'

HENRY's break with Rome, with all its consequences, has been called the Reformation. This word generally implies a change for the better, and is not strictly accurate in this particular case.

The legal sanction for the rupture with Rome had been given by Acts of Parliament. The very fact that Henry had thought it advisable to get the support of Parliament for his plans meant that the power and authority of this talking-club were enormously increased. It must be remembered also that many Members of Parliament, both Lords and Commoners, were enriched beyond the dreams of avarice by the plunder of the Church. A new class of plutocratic landlords came into being, and they and their sons began to get their hands on political power by using Parliament to muzzle the king. The great aristocratic families which controlled Parliament for three hundred years afterwards, almost to our own day, were not descendants of the Norman conquerors: most of them owed their origin to the objectionable profiteers and plunderers who fattened on the Church's lost wealth. Oliver Cromwell, for instance, was one of them.

The rise to power of newly rich landlords and financiers led to sweeping social changes which soon affected the ploughman and the town labourer. The grasping scoundrels who took over the confiscated Church lands were no respecters of tenant-rights. There were evictions, enclosures and extortionate rental demands, which provoked an armed rebellion in Norfolk. The Government was forced to interfere to protect tenants, but when at last the Government fell completely into the hands of the landlords there was no appeal except to their humanity.

In the towns, the guilds which enforced good standards of work and reasonable prices were despoiled like the Church. Many of them had large funds subscribed by members for religious or charitable purposes. These funds were now confiscated, nominally to be used in building grammar schools. Most of the cash, however, found its way into the pockets of 'reforming' landlords and corrupt officials. The old idea, fostered by the Church, of a just price for an article of standard workmanship, was quietly forgotten. The way was paved for unrestricted competition and capitalism, under which the true merchant's policy was to make an article as shoddily as he dared and to sell it for as high a price as he could get. Here again the Government, as long as it remained royal, tried to mitigate the worst effects of the change by passing Acts of Apprentices designed to ensure that every workman was properly trained for his job, and that he got a good living wage for doing it. Yet, as the Reformation carried with it the decay of monarchy, the kings gradually lost the power to enforce these laws; and in the sixteenth century began the long process which ended in the great bulk of the English people becoming wage-earners insecure in their jobs, with no reserves of property and a horrible sapping dread of unemployment, while most of the country's wealth fell into the hands of a tiny fraction of the people.

The confiscation of the Church's property had another troublesome result which the bold Henry had not foreseen. The monasteries and abbeys, which had held their farms and money in trust for the public, had previously solved the questions of poverty, vagabondage and unemployment. When they ceased to function, the workless man became a menace to the public, and ferocious tramps swarmed on the highroads. In these circumstances a Poor Law was passed making each parish responsible for the support of its old people and unemployables. We owe the Workhouse and the Overseers of the Poor to the Reformation. While the profiteers grew fat on the plunder of the Church, the ratepayer footed the bill.

The English break with Rome was entirely political in character. Henry VIII ('Defender of the Faith') was the last man to want changes in doctrine. He thought all Protestants were heretics, and had no patience with them. Nevertheless, once the Pope was out of the way there was an opening for the ideas of the German and Swiss Protestant leaders, Luther and Calvin. Now however sound the reasons for these ideas, however noble and sincere their conception, they could be very easily used by unscrupulous men to serve as a mask for inhumanity, greed, selfishness and cruelty. Protestantism is the creed of individualism in religion. It therefore had attractions for everyone who, for his own reasons, wanted to have individualism in trade and industry and politics, for everyone who wanted to make profits without any restriction in the interests of the

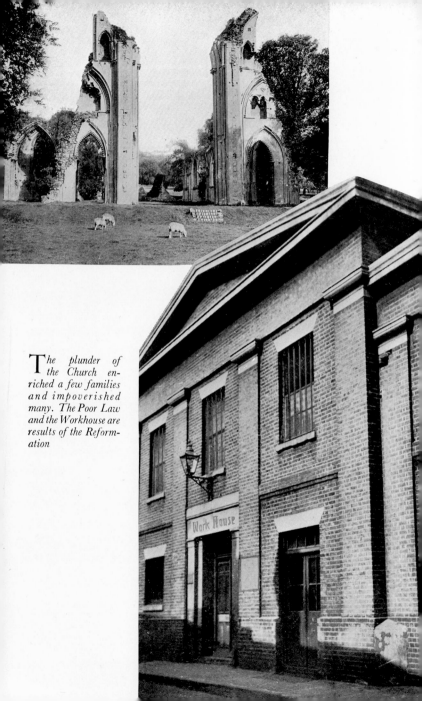

*T*he plunder of the Church enriched a few families and impoverished many. The Poor Law and the Workhouse are results of the Reformation

community at large; who wanted to employ labour without any restrictions as to the wages he must pay; who wanted to have political power without any restrictions in the interests of the public at large. For these reasons the pushing men who had become rich at the expense of the Church found a powerful appeal in the Protestant attitude of mind. Another obvious motive influenced their conduct: a permanent reunion with the Catholic Church might have meant the forfeit of their ill-gotten wealth.

This is not an indictment of Protestantism. It is merely a plain statement of the fact that when the Catholic Church was abandoned, a complete system of regulations for honest trading, humane employment, and political discipline was broken up. Before a new system of State regulation could be permanently established, the profiteers and opportunists had begun to seize political power under the cloak of Protestant ideas. They were only a small proportion of those who became sincere converts to the reforming sects; but they were powerful because of their wealth.

It may reasonably be asked why a nation which had been solidly Catholic submitted to wholesale conversion. The answer is that the change was gradual, taking more than a hundred years (in fact, it was not complete until 1689); that great armed rebellions by Catholics and by the poor were defeated; that the new nobility took care to support anti-Catholic teaching; and that a long national war with Spain, which was enthusiastically followed by the whole people, led everyone to couple Catholicism with the national enemy, as something tyrannous, cruel, bloodthirsty and rapacious.

'God Blew and they were Scattered'

THERE were many mixed motives for the English war with Spain. Henry VIII's eldest daughter Mary (called 'Bloody Mary' because she killed Protestant leaders as her father and sister killed Catholics) was married to Philip of Spain, but died too soon to do much good. Her sister Elizabeth, who then became queen, was much too cunning for the pale fanatical Spaniard, who controlled the great Catholic revival of the sixteenth century. She pretended to be on the best of terms with him while her piratical skippers, of whom Sir Francis Drake was the most famous, made a fat living by waylaying Spanish galleons homeward bound from South America with cargoes of gold and silver. Philip was unwilling to go to war, because his hands were full with the Protestant rebellion in the Netherlands which Elizabeth covertly encouraged. Yet when Drake, in a fit of exuberance, sailed into Cadiz harbour and 'singed the King of Spain's beard', Philip had to retaliate. The Spanish Armada was an attempt to conquer England for the Catholic faith. It was hopelessly defeated by English gunnery, English seamanship, and English weather. Even the English paid tribute to the weather as an ally. 'God blew, and they were scattered' was the Elizabethan way of putting it. It was a momentous victory. The greatest Catholic power, the strongest military and naval nation of the time had been shot to pieces by English pirates, smugglers, and fishermen. It was like the victories of the Boer farmers over the crack troops of the British Empire in 1900. The conceit of the English people knew no bounds. The hold of Protestantism was confirmed.

How the 'Reformation' Poisoned Anglo-Irish Relations

In proportion as the English loathed and feared the Spaniards, the strongest soldiers of the time, they disliked, despised and maltreated the Irish, a disorganized Catholic nation which had fallen into their power.

91

If the English had remained Catholic, or if the Irish had become Protestant, the two nations in the course of time might have shaken down into partnership. As it was, the Reformation split them for centuries, perhaps for ever. Their difference was no longer a difference in social conditions; it had become a difference in civilization, in habits of thought, in conscience and belief.

Henry VIII had done his best to conquer the whole of Ireland and to give all its people the benefit of English law—a privilege previously accorded only to English settlers. But by the time of his daughter Elizabeth, Protestant power had advanced so far that the Mass was forbidden in Ireland. The Pope promptly absolved Elizabeth's Catholic subjects from their allegiance to her, and three Irish rebellions resulted, the first under Shane O'Neill, the second under Desmond, the third under Hugh O'Neill, who very nearly succeeded in driving the English out of the island.

The Government's measures after these rebellions were hardly calculated to conciliate the Irish. A large army was poured into the country and its wages were not paid. The soldiers lived on theft by violence, and on the whole there was little to choose between them and the infamous Black and Tans of 1920.

Secondly, the English Government, having

confiscated Church lands, followed up the policy by confiscating many Irish farms and putting in English tenants. This was done on a comparatively small scale by Elizabeth in the province of Munster. It was copied by James I in Ulster, where the Scottish immigrants have rooted themselves. It was done on an unprecedented scale by the great patriot, liberal statesman, rebel and regicide, Oliver Cromwell. For over two hundred years the consistent policy of all English Governments, royal or republican, Tory or Whig, liberal or conservative, was to strangle Irish nationalism, lame Irish trade, frustrate Irish energy and persecute Irish religion. Only the threat of force could extort any concessions from the English exploiters.

The favourite pastime of sentimental patriots is to brood over the history of their country's wrongs, to denounce the oppressors and glorify the rebels. The sensible man, knowing that no nation is better or worse than another, will try to find in history the cause of national misunderstandings. Once you have grasped the character of the English Reformation you have the key to the Anglo-Irish problem: you realize why Ireland and England, though they may become peaceful neighbours, cannot be intimate friends.

The Spacious Days of Great Elizabeth

ONE curious result of the Reformation was that it led to an alliance between England and Scotland, and ultimately to the union of the two countries. If it had not been for the Reformation, the British Empire might never have acquired its strong Scottish accent, moneylenders might have retained their Oriental patronymics, and Canada might never have been kilt-conscious.

In the sixteenth century both countries were under petticoat rule—the 'monstrous regiment of women'. In England was Queen Elizabeth, the brilliant foxy-haired schemer, who managed to keep her own end up with the ambitious English Parliament. She did her level best to make the religious settlement include everybody, and on the whole she was very successful. But in spite of all she could do, in spite of her immense personal popularity and her astonishing diplomatic victories, a large number of the English remained Catholic, particularly in the North.

In Edinburgh was Mary Queen of Scots, half a Frenchwoman by birth, wholly French by education, and a devoted Catholic. She was a passionate woman, impetuous, wilful and imprudent. Intellectually and morally she was inferior to Elizabeth, who allied herself to the Scottish

94

Protestants. These gentlemen, having plundered the Church in Scotland, acquired a high standard of conduct and finally expelled their queen for her misdemeanours. Mary fled to England for sanctuary, and was promptly made a State prisoner. She remained under guard for nineteen years, and as long as she lived she was a source of danger to her unwilling hostess Elizabeth, because the English Catholics were incessantly plotting on behalf of Mary against their own queen. It was an awkward position for Elizabeth, who felt that she would be letting down the whole class of royalty if she saved her skin by putting Mary to death. Force of circumstances made kings and queens very class-conscious in those days. However, at the end Elizabeth ratted on her class and Mary was beheaded.

This was the beginning of bad times for the English kings. When Elizabeth died she was succeeded by James of Scotland, son of the murdered Mary of Scots. To all appearance he was in a powerful position: the first King of England, Wales, Scotland and Ireland. Yet within fifty years his son King Charles was beheaded as Mary had been.

How the 'Reformation' ruined the Kings

To understand the sequence of events which led to the decapitation of King Charles I and the transfer of political power from the throne to the plutocrats, we must analyse the political ideas which the Reformation spawned in great variety.

James I, whose Scottish love of argument and logic-chopping was unrestrained by Scottish horse-sense, conceived the Reformation as a wise movement specially designed in the interest of kings. He reasoned that after the break with Rome, the King of England became the Pope of England as well, and therefore had a 'Divine Right' to rule without restrictions of any sort, in the interests of the people as a whole. In James's view, only the king could judge what the interests of the people really were.

This view was repugnant to the rich landowners, who felt that James had entirely missed the drift of the Reformation. The logical consequence of the Reformation, to their way of thinking, was that the men who had become rich by plundering the Church should now become powerful by destroying the monarchy.

It was quite obvious that everyone could interpret the Reformation to his own advantage. There were inspired prophets both for the king's view and for the landowner's view. The great Protestant Luther was a firm supporter of the royal power. When the German peasants revolted, Luther's advice to the princes was short and lucid. 'Kill, slay, stab, burn,' he said simply.

On the other hand the equally great Protestant Calvin taught that the power which formerly belonged to the priests should really belong to the congregation. Many landowners began to incline towards Calvin's view. They saw the king claiming priestly power; they saw themselves in Parliament as the king's congregation. They began to clamour for freedom, by which they meant freedom for rich men from interference by the king. They supported their attitude by liberal quotations from the Bible, which in the reign of James I was translated into lovely English. Literary style has its own peculiar dangers. Many English squires got grand passages of the Bible by heart, and always had an apt quotation to justify their own actions and condemn the actions of others.

The struggle between king and Parliament, in which each party believed itself to be on the side of the angels, began with a sordid quarrel about money. The king, in his attempts to regulate trade and employment, to administer equal justice to all, and to provide a strong navy, was put to heavy expense. In the old days, when the

G

97

duties of royalty were less exacting, this expense would have been met out of the revenue of the royal estates and out of the customs duties. But since the metal market had been flooded with silver from America, the value of money had sunk, and the king was unable to make ends meet from his own rent roll. When he tried to raise taxes, the Parliament opposed him with the energy of which all rich men are capable when their pockets are threatened. To take one instance, the king tried to raise ship-money to keep the navy in repair. The tax was strenuously resisted by keen M.P.s who would rather expose the country to foreign invasion than admit the king's right to levy taxes.

Looking back on this unedifying contest between king and Parliament, it must be remembered that Parliament represented only the propertied classes, and was quite unhampered by any democratic checks. The main concern of M.P.s was to protect their own pockets. In the same way, if a modern Parliament represented only the motoring classes, we should have no tax on petrol.

The only representative man in the country, the only man who had to think for rich and poor alike, was the king. The Parliament was only a hindrance. In these circumstances Charles I decided to do without Parliament. He appointed strong royal officers for each district to see that justice was properly administered. If Charles had not tried to make the Church government as orderly as the civil government, he might have come to a good working solution of his political problems, in England at least.

As it was, his desire to strengthen the 'Established Church' led to a Scottish rebellion, the lowland Scots being dour Presbyterians. This was followed by a rebellion among the Catholic Irish, who had been badly handled by Charles's officers. The Irish rebels professed loyalty to the Crown, and asked only for liberty of conscience and stability of land tenure. The English Parliament, called together at last to supply the need for immediate cash in face of these emergencies, was found to be sharply divided between those who wanted power for themselves and those who held to the tradition of monarchy. In 1642 the trouble came to a head, and the Civil War began which was to put Oliver Cromwell in power.

The Curse of Cromwell

AT first the Civil War went in favour of the Royalists. Their cavaliers, under the dashing leadership of Prince Rupert, were more than a match for the rebel levies. Unfortunately, at the critical moment of the war, Oliver Cromwell got control of the rebel forces. This crafty squire happened to be a born cavalry leader and martinet. He was able, with the wealth of the seditious landowners, to offer attractive pay to troopers and pikemen; but it was his inborn military talent that enabled him to drill them into a conquering army. Many of them (called 'Roundheads' and 'Puritans' by later historians) were vagrants, gaolbirds, or ne'er-do-well young tosspots. Yet by lavish use of money and by the force of his own personality, Cromwell made them the instrument of victory; with their support he was able to behead the king and rise to supreme power as Protector.

Exactly what he protected is a mystery. He did not protect Parliament; he turned it out. When one of his officers went to eject the more obstinate M.P.s, their spokesman said: 'We are seeking the Lord.' 'Then you can seek him elsewhere,' replied the waggish soldier, 'for to my certain knowledge he has not been here these many years.'

Nor did Cromwell protect the Irish, who remained obstinate loyalists. His invasion was marked by the wholesale massacre of civilians, and was followed by plague and famine. Even to-day 'the Curse of Cromwell' is a horrible oath in Ireland. Confiscations took place on a huge scale; this was natural enough, because Cromwell's own wealth was inherited from the plunder of the Catholic Church in England a hundred years before. When Cromwell came to Ireland, two-thirds of the land was owned by Catholics; when he left, two-thirds was in the hands of English Protestants, appropriately called 'undertakers'. These new Cromwellian landowners, the ancestors of the Anglo-Irish nobility, were mostly of humble origin. Their ranks included blacksmiths, tinkers, cobblers and grocers. Some of their descendants have returned to England as journalists.

As for Cromwell's government of England, it was a sorry imitation of the late king's rule, and a good deal more despotic. Parliament having been shot out of the way like so much rubbish, the country was governed by military force. Even the extreme Puritans of the Left Wing reviled the great Protector; they called him the Man of Sin, the Beast, the Old Dragon. When he died, the nation sighed with relief, and called back Charles II to be king in place of his martyred father.

The End of the English Catholics

OF all the English kings, Charles II is the most likeable. His father's career had shown him the folly of being too conscientious; his exile had taught him the art of making himself pleasant. A king with a sense of proportion is so rare as to be a continual puzzle to his subjects. Cool, imperturbable, adroit and charming, Charles was able to baffle his Parliamentary opponents and to get his own way in the end. His foreign policy showed great originality. A powerful group of politicians favoured a war with the Catholic King of France, Louis XIV. Louis, who disliked the prospect of an English war while he was up to the chin in Continental troubles, bribed Charles to keep England at peace. As this had been Charles's intention all along, this was a good stroke of business. A king who gets paid for not shedding the blood of his subjects is worthy of respect.

The most significant incident of Charles II's reign was the 'Popish Plot'. This was the invention of a horrible ruffian named Titus Oates, who infuriated the mob with lying stories about plots to massacre the Protestants. Defoe, the author of *Robinson Crusoe*, said that at this time there were a hundred thousand stout countrymen ready to fight to the death against popery, without knowing whether popery was a man or a horse. The truth of this was proved when Charles died with a jest on his lips and was succeeded by his brother James.

James II was a strong Catholic, but had none of his brother's charm or dexterity. He attempted to benefit the English Catholics by introducing a system of religious toleration in the apparent interests of all nonconformists; tried to undo the Cromwellian confiscations in Ireland; and began to establish a standing army. Unfortunately he made many mistakes in detail, and managed to set everyone of importance against him. It was in these circumstances that a group of Reformation noblemen began to intrigue with James's son-in-law, William of Orange. Dutch William was in the thick of a war with France, and badly needed the help of English money and English troops. He therefore crossed to England, having arranged that his father-in-law should be deserted by the troops. James had no option but to run away, and he bungled even this performance. This Dutch invasion is usually called The Glorious Revolution of 1688.

The Glorious Revolution and its Infamous Effects

THE Revolution transferred the reality of political power from the king to a few wealthy Protestant families. These families controlled the Parliament by corruption, and they controlled the king through Parliament. They ruled England, with few checks or intermissions, for 150 years. They called themselves Whigs; their opponents, who favoured the restoration of popular monarchy, were called Tories. The Whigs were the predecessors of the Liberal party, the Tories of the Conservative party. Between them they played a pretty game of battledore and shuttlecock until the last Great War.

The modern British Empire is founded on the work of the rich Whigs. Their ranks included a surprising number of acute and able men of affairs, and even some conscientious ones. In point of wit, style, appearance, education, manners, oratory, breeding, and ability in office, they were undoubtedly superior to the members of a present-day Parliament. This was because they were hereditary legislators, born and bred to rule, and rich enough to be individual and independent, whereas the conditions of modern politics can attract only the mediocrity, the time-server, and the second-rate man. Yet there is a shadow on the most brilliant achievements of the Whigs. They were responsible neither to the Church, nor the king, nor the people. They were responsible only to their own class. Thus though they maintained a rigid code of honour among themselves, there was no overriding code of morality to control their actions in the interests of the people. They were no less good-natured than any other class of men at any time; but when good nature clashed with self-interest, self-interest won.

They introduced a modified system of religious toleration (which excluded the Catholics as a matter of course), but they allowed the national Church to become a class institution, alienated from the people, and with its better-paid posts filled with the younger sons of influential families or their toad-eating friends.

They originated modern banking and credit, establishing the National Debt and the Bank of England. Thus they paved the way financially for the great industrialists who, by taking advantage of the invention of the steam engine, were to transform England from an agricultural country into the workshop of the world; but they made no provision for the welfare of the labourers whom the industrialists employed. In the same way, when improvements in farming were discovered, the Whig landlords passed private bills through

Parliament to enable them to enclose the common land which really belonged to the whole village. But for these acts of legalized theft the modern English farm labourer might still be a thriving peasant instead of a poverty-stricken hack.

The Whigs, though they were great land-owners, had a strong commercial streak. They fought wars on behalf of English trade, and con-quered large areas in India and the Americas which are now painted red on the map. It is true that the French war into which Dutch William forced the English was mainly a Continental affair, and partly religious in character. The French were heavily defeated in a series of pitched battles by the astounding Duke of Marl-borough, the greatest soldier and diplomat that England ever produced. As her share of the spoils of victory, England received Newfoundland, Nova Scotia, Hudson's Bay, Gibraltar, Minorca, and the right of transporting slaves to South America. Other conquests came with later wars.

In Imperial policy, the Whigs, unlike the Liberals, were great protectionists. They tried to regulate trade with the colonies by making the colonists buy all their manufactures from Eng-land. This policy broke down when the American colonies successfully rebelled.

Ireland during the Whig rule was regarded in

the light of a colony. The Irish had supported James II, and as the price of peace Dutch William had agreed to religious freedom. He broke his promise; Catholics were persecuted with renewed vigour. But the Catholics were not the only sufferers under the lash of the Whigs. The Protestants in Ireland had founded a flourishing woollen industry; the Whigs thought it might compete with Yorkshire, and therefore destroyed it without compunction. The tide of Irish emigration began. A bitter hatred of England was sown in America.

Scotland, not being a conquered country, escaped this fate. The Whigs feared an independent country so close at hand, and in 1707 they devised the United Kingdom of Great Britain. A great number of Scots crossed the Border and never looked back. This was the most satisfactory result of the Revolution of 1688.

English historians have called the Whig seizure of power The Glorious Revolution. To many people this will seem an abuse of language, but it must be remembered that England's greatest writers depended on Whig patronage to get a sale for their books.

Corruption of Parliament

DUTCH WILLIAM, having dragged England into a Continental war, was succeeded by his sister-in-law Queen Anne. It was in her reign that the incomparable Marlborough, 'the handsome Englishman', won his stupendous victories over the French. He never lost a battle. He had the coolness, the intrepidity, the lack of sentiment and the certainty of aim which are found only in the born conqueror. His victories, leading to the acquisition of overseas possessions in America and the Mediterranean, secured the Protestant power in England, so that the attempts of James II's Catholic descendants to regain the throne were doomed to failure. In 1715 the Old Pretender tried his luck with a rebellion in the Scottish Highlands, and in 1745 Bonny Prince Charlie repeated the experiment. Each time the vested interests of the Protestants were strong enough to crush the insurrections.

Queen Anne being dead (a fact which is still a subject of comment), she was succeeded by her cousin George I, a German vulgarian who could not speak English. His son George II, a goggle-eyed braggart, was also a complete foreigner. This made it all the easier for the great Whig landlords to control the Government. The German kings did not even attend Cabinet meetings. In these circumstances the Whig leader, Sir Robert Walpole, was for more than twenty years (until 1742) the real ruler of England. He was a fox-hunting Norfolk landowner with a great capacity for drink and for figures. He and his drinking friends controlled Parliament by bribery and corruption. Many of the Whig noblemen had powerful financial interests in Parliamentary boroughs, and simply nominated their friends and parasites as M.P.s. When an independent man got into the House of Commons, his criticism of the Government could generally be silenced by the gift of an official job with no duties and a high salary. The saying that 'every man has his price' is usually credited to Walpole, who only differed from the corrupt politicians of modern America in his avoidance of claptrap and democratic jargon, and his administrative ability. He was a competent financier: in fact, he owed his rise to power to the fact that he kept his head in the speculative orgy of 1721, commonly called the South Sea Bubble, when even the craftiest gamblers burned their fingers like the demented financiers of Wall Street in the crash of 1929.

Walpole's Government ended in another war with France, but by that time he had made Parliament supreme, so that whoever wanted to rule England in the future must be prepared to transfer the revenue of State appointments into the itching palms of rapacious M.P.s. The iniquitous system was firmly grounded. Neither the king nor the people could alter it.

Decay of the English Church

THE Church, like the Parliament, became corrupt in the period of Whig rule. No doubt in the sleepy villages there were still conscientious poor clergymen like Fielding's Parson Adams (who drank small beer in the kitchen of the manor house) and Goldsmith's Vicar of Wakefield. But the clerical jobs with fat stipends went to men of good family or good connections, and bishops were appointed for almost any reason except the clinching reasons of sincerity and fitness for the post. In fact, there were bishops who never visited the sees over which they ruled. There were many comfortable clergymen, like Parson Woodforde, who thought far more of gluttonous meals, wine, card-parties and fox-hunting than of their clerical duties. Many parsons were extravagant drunkards. Among the fashionable set, religion became bad taste. This point of view was well expressed by a Whig leader, Lord Melbourne, who lived on into Queen Victoria's reign. Happening to be in church, he found himself listening to an enthusiastic sermon. 'Things have come to a pretty pass,' he said, 'when religion is allowed to invade the sphere of private life.'

Most of the regular clergy were too fond of comfort to let religion invade their own private lives, and were therefore unlikely to interfere with their parishioners. The poorer classes began to imitate their betters. They could not afford to drink port wine, but they could afford gin and strong beer, which became very cheap. Drunkenness became a national hobby, as Hogarth's horrible drawings attest.

In these circumstances a number of irregular clergymen, notably Wesley and Whitefield, began a revivalist campaign among the poor and the middle classes. Wesley delivered fifteen sermons a week for fifty years on end. He founded the Wesleyan Methodists, a religious body which attracted and satisfied many active spirits who might otherwise have become embittered agitators. Tradesmen, mechanics, labourers and miners found a new interest in life and morals through Methodism. They were great hymn-singers and philanthropists, with liberal views on prison administration, slavery, and religious missions to foreign parts. In the course of time every religious movement attracts hypocrites who cloak their petty dishonesty under high moral professions. But this development takes place only when the movement has ceased to be enterprising and reforming and stimulating, and has become conventional and narrowly respectable. During Wesley's lifetime (he died in 1790) his followers were among the most sensible, honest, and productive people in England. It was largely their influence which, at the time of the French Revolution, prevented a similar rebellion in England.

Methodism was essentially a lower-class movement. The Duchess of Buckingham was once invited by a friend to attend one of Whitefield's sermons. Her refusal would have been endorsed by most of her circle. 'It is monstrous', she said, 'to be told you have a heart as sinful as the common wretches that crawl on the earth; and I cannot but wonder that your ladyship should relish any sentiments so much at variance with high rank and good breeding.'

Chatham the Stage-Manager of Imperialism

WHILE John Wesley was indefatigably stumping the country preaching revivalist sermons, a figure equally curious, equally domineering, and equally typical of the best English gentry stepped into the shoes of Walpole as leader of Parliament.

This was the elder Pitt, the first Earl of Chatham, a former Army officer with an unreasoning love of England, terrific self-confidence, and a theatrical sense which would have fitted him for the chief part in a popular melodrama. He loathed Parliamentary corruption, and considered that he had a mandate from the English people whose common prejudices he shared. He left the work of bribery and palm-oiling to mediocre colleagues; for himself, he ostentatiously refused to take more money than he was officially entitled to —a principle which at once distinguished him from other politicians. By means of make-up and consummate showmanship he built up a tremendous uncritical popularity among all classes, including the vast numbers who were totally unrepresented in Parliament.

It was in the conduct of the seven years' war with France (1756 to 1763) that Chatham made his most spectacular strokes. He had a talent for choosing good men, and he supported his choices with passionate conviction. Under his direction England conquered the French in Canada and India, and saved the colonies which afterwards revolted to form the United States of America.

He was the greatest English war minister who ever lived. He made his country victorious in three continents.

The Indian Empire was one product of Chatham's French war. The glory of its acquisition was offset by the shamelessness with which it was exploited by English profiteers, who came home as millionaires. The scandal became so notorious that the Whig politicians staged a great trial of the Indian governor, Warren Hastings. They held that conquered peoples should be given the best government that could be got for love or money, and not exposed to oppression or exploitation. This sound idea might well have been applied to the oppressed Irish as well as the oppressed Indians. In politics, however, charity seldom begins at home.

Why the Americans Rebelled

THE two German kings of England were succeeded by a third George who 'gloried in the name of Briton'. He was a robust, well-meaning, respectable young man, with a strong vein of patriotism; and he soon determined to take a leaf out of Chatham's book, and to control the Parliament in the interests of the people.

The only way of controlling Parliament was by corruption. As a great number of official jobs depended on royal patronage, George found that he could meet the Whig landlords on their own ground. By a system of discriminate bribery he was able to form a strong party of Tory M.P.s who called themselves the 'King's Friends'.

Unfortunately 'Farmer George' had none of Chatham's genius. Chatham had a dramatic imagination and a knack of attracting the limelight; George had no gift for rousing the enthusiasm of his followers. Chatham had a hawk-eye for good officers and assistants, even when their strong points were offset by obscurity or eccentricity; and when he had appointed a man, he supported him up to the hilt. But George had the mediocre man's fancy for mediocrities, and was obstinate rather than resolute in his national policy.

While George was thus sowing his political wild oats the North American colonists broke into rebellion. They had been loyal enough while they needed English troops to repel the menace of French invasion; but when that danger was past, and part of the bill for military expenses was presented to them for payment, they promptly repudiated their obligations to England. They were led by George Washington, a fine old English gentleman of the Cromwell breed who accurately represented the American view, which was in fact nothing more than the view of Cromwell's friends who had refused to pay Ship-money a century before. The English generals were mishandled and badly supported by George's War Office, and the French declared war too. Though the Americans won on land, the French were smashed at sea. In 1783 the United States were recognized as independent. Later historians have exaggerated the contemporary feeling of dismay at the loss of the colonies. No doubt many of the Americans were unpleasantly conceited and bumptious. When Doctor Johnson said: 'I am willing to love all mankind, except an American', he was expressing a very popular view.

The American War led to a queer settlement in Ireland, where the Protestants raised a strong volunteer army ostensibly to repel foreign invaders. The existence of such an army was not entirely agreeable to the English rulers, and they decided to let Ireland have an independent Parliament again, and to remove the restrictions on Irish trade.

This Irish Parliament, under the leadership of Grattan, was entirely Protestant in composition. It had three hundred members, two-thirds of whom were returned by less than one hundred rich Protestants who attempted with ludicrous results to stimulate Irish trade by putting a tariff on English goods.

The unfortunate Catholics were as badly off as before, and had to enlist English pressure to get the relief measure of 1793, which enfranchised the Catholics, gave them the right to own land, and allowed them to act as jurymen. For the mass of the Irish people Grattan's Parliament was only a bad joke, and it died of its own follies in 1800.

The French Revolution bred Diehards in England

MIDWAY through the rollicking life of Grattan's Parliament, the bombshell of the French Revolution burst among the rulers of Europe. Its splinters landed in other countries than France. England and Ireland felt the shock equally with Austria, Germany and Italy.

The French revolutionists, like the modern Bolshevists, were not content with a local victory. They set themselves to propagate their ideas internationally, and did this very effectually without the help of wireless. The effect in England was disastrous. George III's Prime Minister, the younger Pitt, had been considering schemes of Parliamentary reform. The propaganda of revolution made him recoil violently from all thoughts of reform. Most of the Whigs, under the Irish orator Edmund Burke, followed his lead and played for safety. The self-interest of the rich combined with the sentimentalism of monarchy to drive the English into war with the French regicides. Only a small section of the Whigs welcomed the Revolution and tried to apply its ideas to English institutions. Under the denunciations of the Conservative diehards they stuck to the idea of a purified Parliament responsible to the nation, but for many years they were kept in the cold winds of opposition. Charles James Fox, the leader of this fighting minority in Parliament, was the greatest profligate and gambler of the age; but he deserves to be remembered as an English aristo-crat who sacrificed his chances of political power for the sake of an unselfish idea.

It was a disaster for England that the French Revolution should drive her statesmen into re-action and repression at the very moment when political and social reorganization was urgently necessary. New problems had come to light with the invention of steam-driven machinery, the improvement of transport and road construction, and the triumphant success of new methods of farming. All these developments might have been expected to produce a greater level of happiness and comfort among the people of England. Actually, however, they resulted in untold misery simply because they were not wisely planned and controlled in the national interest.

How the 'Scum of the Earth' won Waterloo

THIS was how it came about. The English government, having become fiercely re-actionary because of the excesses of the Continental revolutionists, entered on a twenty years' war with France, which became a life-and-death struggle when Napoleon staked everything in a magnificent bid for the mastery of a united Europe.

To keep the war going, the English government, under Pitt, had to tax heavily and to stimulate the output of manufactures and food. The new machines made increased production easily possible, and no obstacles were placed in the way of the great industrialists and manufacturers of the North. There were no restrictions as to the wages or hours or age of workers; women and children might be made to work sixteen hours a day at starvation pay; and the derelict towns of our modern industrial areas, with their acres of miserable hovels, are the result of this negation of national policy. The factory operatives were not even given the chance of banding themselves together to demand higher wages. Trade unions were prohibited and unionists were in danger of being deported like convicts to penal settlements abroad.

The workers for the new industries came from the country. Population had grown, and it was essential that English farms should produce more food. Experiments by wealthy landowners had shown that the old three-field system of farming, in which every villager had his own strips of land and the right to pasture his cattle on the common land, was not calculated to get the full value out of the land. In these circumstances the landlords passed private bills through Parliament enabling them to enclose village fields and commons and to evict the villagers with very little in the way of compensation. The English countryman, hitherto a small farmer on his own account, became a poaching, underpaid labourer or drifted to the towns to work in the new factories. Even the landlords, as the war went on, recognized that the farm labourers could not keep body and soul together on the wages they received; but instead of raising wages, the magistrates began a degrading system of parish relief, or local doles, which degraded the countryman to the position of a beggar.

The English country man has come down in the world. As a peasant proprietor he was a small farmer on his own account until powerful landlords enclosed the common lands, and forced him on the rates or drove him to the factory towns as an unskilled labourer

But the landlords and manufacturers flourished, and the war against Napoleon went on. The English Navy, manned largely by kidnapped sailors who sometimes mutinied because of bad food and maltreatment, was mistress of the sea after Trafalgar, the last and greatest victory of Lord Nelson. The English army, commanded by the Duke of Wellington, a Protestant Irishman who called his troops 'the scum of the earth', beat the French in Spain and finally helped to crush Napoleon at Waterloo.

Self-Made Laws for Self-Made Men

AT the end of the Napoleonic wars, when other nations were licking their wounds, England emerged as the supreme industrial nation, the Workshop of the World. The manufacturers and shopkeepers, more wealthy than ever before, began to challenge the political power of the landowners. They allied themselves to the great Whig families, while the Tories who had conducted the war began a series of strategic retreats under Wellington and Peel.

The political and economic ideas of the English manufacturers and tradesmen have been grouped under the name of *laisser-faire*. *Laisser-faire* meant freedom for manufacturers to impose their own terms on workmen and farmers alike. It meant cut-throat competition in trade, with the least possible amount of governmental regulation in the interests of the nation as a whole.

In short, *laisser-faire* meant the abandonment of all attempts at national planning. It resulted in the tenure of political power by financiers, industrialists and tradesmen, who acquired most of the wealth of the community; in the decline of English farming, which had previously been able to feed the whole country; and in the haphazard creation of a vast town population, poorly paid, wretchedly housed, and in constant fear of unemployment.

Yet it would be unjust to regard the manufacturers as unmitigated rascals. Most of them were self-made men who had taken advantage of mechanical inventions and found themselves suddenly rich. Like all self-made men, they attributed their success to the wrong causes. They minimized the extent to which sheer luck or an instinct for getting the better of rivals or a knack of exploiting the weakness of others had influenced their careers. Instead, they traced their fortunes to their own sobriety, honesty and industry. The same faults of self-analysis have been observed in modern millionaires. The viewpoint of the manufacturers was expressed later in a book called *Self-Help*, which gave many anecdotes about poor boys who rose to fame and fortune by following the precepts of the copybooks.

It seemed to the manufacturers that any workman, if he had enough grit and ambition, could be as successful as themselves. They thought that every man should fight for his own hand, and that no quarter should be asked or given. They considered themselves the Apostles of Freedom because they advocated the removal of all restrictions on industrial and commercial competition. Thus though they gave workmen a Parliamentary vote, they fought tooth and nail against Trade Unions which attempted to get better wages and better conditions for workmen. Though they abolished negro slavery in the West Indies and South Africa, they were bitter enemies of the philanthropists who proposed that women and tiny children in England should not be allowed to work more than twelve hours a day.

Thus the nineteenth-century notion of Freedom, pushed to its logical end, simply meant the absence of national organization. Employers were free to slave-drive their workers, lashing them on with the threat of unemployment and starvation. Manufacturers were free to pollute the air with smoke and the rivers with garbage.

Poor miners' women were free to harness themselves like beasts and draw coal-trucks in the pits. Little boys and girls were free to work for sixteen hours a day under the whip of an overseer. Freedom is a comprehensive word, and means different things to different classes of people.

The England of Dickens

THESE notions of freedom flourished on the grave of the old popular monarchy. George III, the last king to take an active hand in the management of Parliament, died in 1820, mad, blind and old. His son George IV, a contemptible lout, has sometimes been called the First Gentleman in Europe; it is to be hoped that he was the last gentleman of that kind in Europe or anywhere else. His brother William IV was an amiable buffoon. Queen Victoria, who came to the throne in 1837 and reigned for more than sixty years, managed to live down the disreputable memory of her predecessors, and by sheer longevity made the monarchy a respectable and convenient figurehead for the Empire.

In the later demented days of George III, political power ebbed away from the throne, and the Parliament, composed of landowners, was supreme.

But as the manufacturers and tradesmen became wealthy and self-confident, they saw the advantages which would accrue if they could wriggle themselves into the House of Commons and make laws on their own account. The landowners, like black-balling members of an exclusive club, were at first unwilling to admit these parvenus; but in 1832 the pressure became too strong and they passed the Great Reform Bill, the effect of which was to open the doors of Parliament to the wealthy middle class: the merchants, the mill owners, the speculative financiers who controlled banks and new railways.

The aim of the new M.P.s was to abolish political regulation of trade, and to prevent humane regulation of industry. The results of these ideas were seen in various ways. For instance, under the old Parliament of landowners it was the custom to regulate colonial trade in the supposed interests both of the colonies and of the mother country; but in 1838, when the Canadians rebelled, a new policy of giving Home Rule to colonies was established so that merchants and manufacturers could trade freely without governmental restrictions. This was the beginning of self-government in the Overseas Dominions, which to-day put tariffs on competing English goods.

This intense hatred of State regulation was

responsible also for the Repeal of the Corn Laws. The Corn Laws were designed to protect the English farmer, and to ensure good prices for English corn, on the theory that no country could be in a really healthy state unless the basic industry of food production was flourishing. The manufacturers, however, having grown richer and therefore more powerful than the farmers, considered that cotton mills and iron foundries in hideous industrial towns were more important than thriving farms in a contented countryside. A cunning agitation against the Corn Laws was engineered by a commercial traveller named Cobden and a mill-owner named Bright; it was so well managed that in 1846 Sir Robert Peel, leader of the Conservatives, repealed the Corn Laws. Cobden and Bright claimed that this would mean cheap bread for everyone, made from cheap foreign corn. The farmers insinuated that Cobden and Bright only wanted to have cheap bread as an excuse for forcing down the wages of mill hands in the North.

Certainly Cobden and Bright were malignant enemies of the great Lord Shaftesbury, a humane and religious man who in spite of bitter opposition tried to protect working women and children from exploitation by factory owners. Other deeply religious people were appalled at the conditions of work in industrial towns; for instance, the parson Charles Kingsley (author of *Westward Ho!*) aided and abetted the trade unionists when they fought for better terms in the first great strike of 1852. That strike failed; but it did not destroy trade unions, as the employers had hoped. In vain they announced a vindictive policy against trade unionists: their callous abuse of economic and political power had become intolerable to all humane people who ever gave a thought to the relations of rich and poor. In the astonishing early days of industrial expansion after the Napoleonic wars, what with railways, steamships, steam engines, canals, metalled roads, and so on, everyone had been dazzled into the illogical belief that progress in the use of machinery must of necessity lead to progress in the material, intellectual and moral condition of the whole people. Yet the idea wore off as people of good feeling and sound sense began to realize that a man with a knack for mechanics and a good head for figures might be more dangerous to the country than a landowner with good traditions. It has often been pointed out that in the novels of Dickens, who lived from 1812 to 1870, we can trace the flight from the glorious self-satisfaction of the early Victorians to the growing doubts of the late Victorians. From the high spirits of

Pickwick and Sam Weller we pass gradually to the corrupt financier of Little Dorrit and the gloom of Our Mutual Friend.

The Uncrowned King and the grand old Spider

DISRAELI, a much less entertaining writer than Dickens, had a surer grasp of the political and economic realities underlying the English position. He pointed out that the English, once a people homogeneous in thought, religion, and habits, had now become divided into two very distinct castes: the ruling caste, controlling money, machines and political power, educated at public schools and holding all the positions which required culture and influence and manners; and the vast, inarticulate, hungry and hopeless class of helots, labourers, or 'wage-slaves', the conditions of whose lives—their housing, their hours of work, their terms of employment, their family life, the upbringing of their children— were dictated by the interests or the fancies of their employers. This was the result of the long process which, starting with the dismemberment of the Church, had led to the seizure of power by rich men at the expense of the old popular monarchy, and to the growth of vast private fortunes which were paid for by the disappearance of the peasant farmers and the enslavement of the working people in the sickening industrial towns which grew like toadstool patches round factories and mines.

In the old days the nation had counted its wealth in terms of the honesty, intelligence, healthiness and independence of its ordinary citizens: but in Victorian times the nation's wealth was counted in the financial profits of its capitalists, employers, and Lombard Street money barons. As a political economist, Disraeli was a follower of Oliver Goldsmith, who had prophesied the future of England in *The Deserted Village*:

> '*Ill fares the land, to hastening ills a prey*
> *Where wealth accumulates, and men decay.*'

Disraeli's aim (however far he fell short of it) was to unite the landowners in interest with the working classes. In 1867 he induced the Conservatives (at that time a party of squires) to give the Parliamentary vote to working men. During his Government which began in 1874 he passed laws for slum clearance, better sanitation, better housing, more freedom for Trade Unions and better conditions in factories.

Disraeli also, by a showy foreign and imperial

policy, tried to rouse the interest of the English people in their world-responsibilities. His troops crushed the Zulus in South Africa, where Gladstone's vacillating policy was shortly afterwards to lead to the first Boer War. In India the Afghans were defeated, and Queen Victoria, by a piece of 'Dizzy's' Jewish showmanship, was made Empress of India.

Disraeli's most consistent, able and dangerous enemy was the 'Grand Old Spider' Gladstone, an aristocrat from Eton and Oxford whose religious attitude, emotional oratory, and belief in freedom for Armenians, Bulgarians, Afghans and other distant races, made him the idol of the English manufacturers and shopkeepers who formed the backbone of the Liberal party, which alternated with the Conservatives in the government of England.

From 1880 to 1890 a third party held the balance between Liberals and Conservatives. This was the Irish Nationalist party, under the leadership of Parnell, the 'uncrowned King of Ireland'. He was the strongest statesman of the age, 'a man of bronze', a born leader and tactician. His genius fused the Irish members at Westminster into a vigorous party with a decisive influence on the government of the whole British Empire. Parnell never permitted his followers to be tamed and befooled as former Irish members had been. He trusted no English politicians further than he could see them. He attracted the financial and moral support of the Irish-Americans and the Irish in England. He demanded two things: Home Rule and fair play for the Irish peasant farmer. It would have been well for England if he had succeeded. Unfortunately at the height of his power he became the co-respondent in a divorce suit. The English Liberals, so long in his power, seized the opportunity to repudiate him on the grounds of propriety and morality, and managed thus to split the Irish Nationalist party. Gladstone's betrayal of Parnell postponed the settlement of the Irish question, and embittered both sides. Though in later years the Irish landlords were bought out in favour of the peasants, it seemed that the prospect of an amicable political settlement was buried with Parnell.

Cecil Rhodes, the South African millionaire, described Parnell as the most sensible and reasonable man he had ever met, and subscribed to the Home Rule funds. Rhodes had many fine ideas but many corrupt helpers, and their activities were largely responsible for the outbreak of the Anglo-Boer war, in which a small body of Dutch farmers held the crack troops of the British Empire at bay for several years. A few years after the war the English Government granted virtual independence to South Africa, thus converting their late enemies into a friendly people. But it needed another war, nearer home, to make them concede independence to the Irish.

The Revival of National Planning

THE turn of the century, with the death of Queen Victoria, the shabby victories of the Boer War, and the beginning of German military and naval aggression, saw the growth of a new temper among the English people. The mass of the population were townsmen who, having been taught to read but not to think, were content to imbibe their political opinions from halfpenny newspapers. Now that they had the vote, their real interest in politics began to decline; they could have a good laugh at the antics of the Suffragettes, but a professional football match was far more to their taste than a political discussion.

Yet all those who were actually concerned in politics had begun to see that the haphazard jerry-built social arrangements of the Victorian age must be patched up somehow, especially as a small group of intellectual Socialists had com-

Our industrial towns are a legacy of the Nineteenth Century, when manufacturers were allowed to build up their businesses without regard for the health and housing of their workers. To-day we are trying to patch up their blunders with Factory Acts, public health measures, unemployment insurance and town-planning

bined with the leaders of the Trade Unions to form the Labour Party in the House of Commons. At last it became recognized that the State must interfere with the private individual for the good of all citizens, as Queen Elizabeth had interfered four hundred years before, and as the Church had interfered before Elizabeth. Thus employers were made increasingly liable for accidents to their workpeople, Labour Exchanges were set up, and a beginning was made for a system of unemployment insurance. Minimum wages were fixed for sweated trades. Poor children were given the chance of getting more than an elementary education, and teachers were better trained. Old Age Pensions were begun. And to meet these new national expenses, new taxes had to be laid on the monied classes, who writhed and squirmed in the effort to escape.

Money had also to be found for the 'Dreadnoughts' which were needed to keep pace with the growing power of the German navy. The life of the British Empire depended on its ability to secure the sea-connections, and England could not afford to have a rival sea-power in Europe. Hence the diplomatic 'conversations' with French and Russian war-staffs to guard against the event of German aggression; hence the British army reforms and Churchill's naval preparations; hence

England's entry into the war of 1914-1918, a desperate fight for existence.

This time there was no Marlborough or Wellingto to lead the English to victory in Flanders; there was no 'Nelson touch' at sea. Millions of men were conscripted, industries were nationalized, borrowed money was spent like water and once again England emerged victorious from the European shambles.

A Nation Once Again

YET there were tragic differences between the England of 1815, when Napoleon was crushed and exiled, and the England of 1918, when the German Emperor was driven from his throne. In each case the Continental bogeyman who threatened English power and prosperity was defeated. But whereas in 1815 England was the only fully-developed industrial nation, with a long lead over her competitors, in 1918 she was one of many. A small professional army and an efficient navy had been enough to guard England against Napoleon; but the war against Germany demanded the sacrifice of all that was best among those of fighting age. For years after the war the government of England was in the hands of old politicians

supported by the profiteers who had made fortunes during the war.

Yet the prospect abroad had never been more
gloomy. The financial supremacy of the world had
passed from London to America, which had
entered the war after much hesitation and made a
good deal of profit out of it. The command of the
sea, once a British monopoly, now had to be
shared between England, America, and Japan.
The Eastern peoples, so long regarded as a market
for English manufactures, had learned to work
their own wage-slaves in their own factories,
largely with the help of English capital at the
expense of English workers. In Russia the
Bolshevist Revolution of 1917 turned a servile
peasantry into an efficient industrialized community. And every nation, to protect its own
industries, built high tariff walls to prevent the
entry of British exports. The channels of world
trade began to choke, and in England, the greatest of exporting countries, the effect was an
immense increase of unemployment.

The European war resulted also in the partition
of Ireland. In 1916 a handful of Sinn Feiners took
advantage of England's difficulties to start a rebellion in Dublin. This was easily suppressed, but
the threat of fighting made the English eager to
give concessions, an attitude which of course

encouraged others to join the Sinn Fein movement. When the Government attempted in 1918 to force conscription on Irishmen, there was an immediate uproar which still further swelled the ranks of Sinn Fein. Thereafter about 2,000 'gunmen' conducted a small private war against the armed police. The Government retaliated by sending over 6,000 English ex-servicemen who, because of their motley garments and canine habits, were called Black and Tans. Of all the blunders committed by the English in Ireland, this was the most shocking and contemptible. Many of the Black and Tans were criminal riffraff, and they robbed and killed in great style. In a few months they achieved a result which had taken Parnell years of effort: they united all Ireland except Ulster against the English Government, which saw the red light and capitulated to the Irish leaders in 1921. The Irish Free State was the result; but its establishment was by no means the end of the Anglo-Irish question, especially as the six North-Eastern counties of Ulster were allowed to stand out and form a Ruritanian principality about the size of Yorkshire.

Towards Home Rule for England

THE English people, however, were no longer passionately interested in the Irish question. The time had come when the oppressed English (as distinct from the oppressed Irish, the oppressed Indians, and the oppressed Africans) demanded a share of the Government's attention. The breakdown of international trade which followed the war resulted in an unemployment roll of two million people, all of them voters who could do much to unseat a Government. In addition, the socialist Labour party had now become the only alternative to the Conservative party. Between 1924 and 1931 there were two Labour Governments under the leadership of Mr. Ramsay MacDonald.

On the whole, however, there was little difference between Conservative and Labour administrations. No intelligent politicians could evade the conclusion that the economic life of the whole community must be planned by the State, as Queen Elizabeth had planned it four hundred years before. Even before the war, owing to the shortcomings of individual capitalists, many sections of social life had passed into the control of government or municipal departments: roads, streets, water supplies, trams, schools and so on were administered by civil servants. Each year since the war has seen an advance towards national or corporate action in place of individual action. A system of insurance for the unemployed has been devised as a safety valve against revolution. Piecemeal housing and town planning schemes have been subsidized by the government. Efforts have been made to regulate and stimulate industry and trade by the erection of protective tariffs, the formation of marketing boards for pigs, milk, potatoes and so on, and the award of subsidies to shipping and agricultural concerns. The Government, following the example of Ireland, has backed the construction of a national electricity system: the gas undertakings had already organized themselves in the interests of the public.

To finance its new activities, the Government is quietly redistributing the national income by means of income tax, surtax and death duties. There is a general levelling-out of incomes, and a greater community of tastes between all classes. In the meantime, free education has been extended so that the public-school monopoly of good government jobs has been broken down, and a large proportion of higher civil servants find their ways to office from state-aided schools and state scholarships at the universities.

Perhaps too late the English will realize once

again that the touchstone of national wealth is not the inflated fortune of the gambling financier, the manufacturer or the shopkeeper, but the intelligence, independence and healthiness of the ordinary citizen. Judging by this standard, we may doubt the optimistic philosophy of English historians who see the story of their country as a rousing tale of progress. The English workman of to-day—the gasfitter, the miner, the navvy, the hopeless lounger outside the Labour Exchange—is of the same stock as the English clansman who sped the plough for a Roman master. His descent goes back to the English peasant farmer of the Middle Ages, when the Church enforced just prices and customary rights, and to the jolly yeoman of Shakespearean days, when the English queen legislated to prevent the poor from exploitation by the rich. His immediate ancestors were the villagers who were evicted from their holdings by powerful landlords and forced to take poor relief, or driven into the industrial towns to tend the machines of the mill owners for sixteen hours a day, or thrust into the coal mines to produce royalties for titled coal owners. The landowners, mill owners and so on, having seized economic and political power and being under no restraint either from the Church or the king, convinced themselves that they could serve the national interest best by piling up fortunes on their own account, without regard to the welfare of their countrymen who hewed the coal, operated the machines, and tilled the land. This absence of beneficial restraint would have been called anarchy in the Middle Ages. In the nineteenth century it was called freedom.

To-day the statesmen of England are working to repair the ravages of nineteenth-century 'freedom'. But they work uncertainly, with one eye on the clock, afraid that the next stroke may be the signal for a new war which will blow Western civilization to smithereens.